Front cover:
G-BKVZ, a Boeing 767-204 operated by Britannia Airways seen on the tarmac at Bristol.
Austin J. Brown/Aviation Picture Library

Back cover:
During the demanding flight development programme for the prototype Boeing 777, it was necessary to demonstrate minimum take-off speed. The tail was protected by a laminated oak skid, and the aircraft is shown just beginning to become airborne from Edwards AFB in California. *Boeing*

**Rolls-Royce RB211-powered British Airways 757-236ER
G-BPED painted in the new colours on approach to
London Heathrow in August 1998.** *Author*

Modern Civil Aircraft: 6
BOEING
757/767/777

Philip Birtles

Ian Allan
PUBLISHING

Third Edition

Contents

First published 1987
Second edition 1992
Third edition 1999

ISBN 0 7110 2665 3

Published by Ian Allan Publishing

an imprint of Ian Allan Publishing Ltd, Terminal House, Shepperton, Surrey TW17 8AS.
Printed by Ian Allan Printing Ltd, Riverdene Business Park, Hersham, Surrey KT12 4RG.

Code: 9906/A2

Below:
Lauda Air of Austria has a total of four Boeing 777s on order. 777-2Z9 OE-LPA was the first to arrive and is seen at the new Kuala Lumpur International Airport on 5 May 1998 soon after it had opened. *Martha Birtles*

Introduction

Since the second edition of this book, published at the end of 1991, major advances have been made in all the following aircraft programmes. The 757 has been developed into the stretched -300 version with the first flight of the new version from Renton in July 1998; the 767 has not only been stretched into the -400 which is currently in the design and engineering stage, but has also been adapted as a freighter and a replacement for the 707 as an AWACS aircraft for Japan; and the 777 has flown and entered service, with the new stretched -300 entering service also.

Below:
Following the break from British Airways, US Airways adopted a new identity. 757-225 N604AU was the 17th 757 built and delivered to Eastern, as N509EA, one of 11 ex-Eastern 757s with the airline. US Airways also operates 23 757s delivered to the airline new. N604AU is on approach to Seatac Airport, which serves Seattle and Tacoma, in May 1998. *Author*

Bottom:
Asiana operates a fleet of 12 767-300ERs plus one 767-300ER Freighter. Boeing 767-38EER HL7264 approaches past the buildings surrounding the now closed Kai Tak airport in April 1998. *Author*

1. Boeing 767 Conception

The design, development and production of a modern jet airliner can take up to 10 years from conception to entry into service. During this critical time when the best ideas are being put into hardware, the market place itself can change, risking the effectiveness of the resulting product. New technology can be introduced to be cost effective in terms of performance, safety, reliability and economy, but with this evolving continually; a point in time has to be set to decide to build the aircraft to the standards available. The aircraft manufacturer, therefore, needs the services of a crystal ball, since no amount of analysis can predict a market situation with a high level of accuracy so far in advance, particularly with its cyclical variations.

In the l960s, Boeing had become well established in the jet airliner market with the Boeing 707 four-jet long-range family of aircraft, including the 720, followed by the trijet Boeing 727 medium-range aircraft, with over 1,500 of the latter being sold worldwide. Then the oil crisis hit a totally unsuspecting world market losing a cheap source of energy. The airlines were hit as hard as anyone, finding that their operating costs had soared out of control almost overnight. The Boeing 747 was entering service, providing a sudden large increase in capacity for the long range services, but having a difficulty in initially filling the seats on highly competitive routes.

During the late 1960s and early 1970s, like many companies in aerospace, Boeing experienced a traumatic downturn in business as a result of the world recession. The peak engineering costs of the Boeing 747 had just passed, to which were added the cancellation effects of the Boeing SST. To save the company, the workforce was cut by two thirds to 36,000 people over a period of three years; but, by the end of the decade, it was able to return to a workforce of 75,000.

It was during this time of stringent economy that the company formulated the New Aircraft Programme within the Commercial Airplane Group at Seattle in the 1970-71 period. The objective was to predict the market requirements for the next 10-15 years, and establish how best to meet the needs, with if necessary a family of

jet airliners, to replace or complement the 707, 727, 737 and 747 jet airliners then in production.

From a whole range of airliner designs examined, Boeing released in August 1971 an artist's impression of what was labelled the 'Boeing 767'. This project had highly swept back wings attached to an area ruled fuselage and a high mounted swept tailplane on a swept fin. The four advanced engines, two mounted on underwing

pylons and two on the rear fuselage, were expected to give the aircraft a cruising speed of Mach 0.98, just avoiding the sonic boom problem. Up to 200 passengers could have been carried.

With their Concorde and Airbus programmes, European countries have become known for international collaboration on major airliner projects, but in fact less obviously, the Boeing airlin-

Above:
The Boeing 757 and 767 were in flight development at the same time, requiring considerable company resources.
All photographs courtesy of Boeing unless otherwise credited

ers are probably just as international, bringing profits eventually to their risk sharing partners worldwide.

The initial layout of the Boeing 751 project, a designation used throughout the evolution of the Boeing 767, was a high augmentor type wing to achieve STOL performance, with a T-tail and four podded engines. It was expected to cruise at Mach 0.8 for 805-1,287km, for service entry in the mid-1970s. In order to achieve STOL performance, blown flaps and direct jet lift systems were also investigated. Deliveries would have been from assembly lines established in Italy and the USA.

The original STOL concept of operating from 2,500ft runways was dropped as totally uneconomic and for a while, the Boeing Aeritalia BA-751 was studied as a QSH (Quiet Short Haul) jet transport intended to operate from readily available 4,000-6,000ft runways. Reduction in engine noise had become a primary requirement, which brought with it increased economy and efficiency. The aim was to operate the new airliner into downtown or secondary airports, because they are normally better placed than major international airports, being closer to the final origin and destination of the majority of air travellers. However, it was seen that there would be major commercial disadvantages by concentrating on airfield performance over all other considerations, and in September 1972 a newly launched advanced airliner programme was announced under the designation 7X7 for the first time, overtaking the QSH studies.

The new objective was to establish the appropriate aircraft to meet the airline requirements from the mid-1970s, while complementing the developments of the existing products. Although work continued on project design under the Boeing drawing number sequence, type 751, the adoption of the 7X7 established the new programme as a firm part of the regular Boeing family.

In early 1973, a number of airlines received presentations on the 7X7 family of related designs, the hope being to try to define at least the most acceptable common initial version by the middle of the year. However, demand for the Boeing 727 began to rise in mid-1973, and it was felt that any decision on a new type might prematurely cut short the market for the existing aircraft. Even the revised target date for launch of the new aircraft by 1 January 1974 for service entry at the end of 1977 was overly optimistic, project development continuing for more than another four years before the 7X7 was finally to emerge as a firm design.

Quietness of operation was still considered a major goal, and the most cost effective ways of achieving the best results were investigated. The new high by-pass fan engines, with their relatively low exhaust velocity, avoided the painful roar of the earlier jet engines, but the installation on the airframe, the acoustic linings, intake and exhaust geometry, all played their part.

Below:
The 767 has a remarkable pedigree, following the 707, 727, 737 and 747 jet airliners into worldwide airline service. The 100th 767 was rolled out at the same time as the 600th 747.

As a medium range twin jet, the 7X7 would require a pair of 40,000-43,000lb-thrust engines, which could be provided by the General Electric CF-6, Rolls-Royce RB211 or Pratt & Whitney JT9D variants. The basic medium range aircraft would be able to carry 140 passengers over some 4,630km. Interest began to grow on longer ranges, which developed from the analysis of the initial airline responses. To achieve this requirement, a three engine layout was considered, one in the tail like the Boeing 727 and the other two in wing pods. Seating would be for about 200 passengers, but the cabin width was not defined, six or seven abreast tourist layouts being considered, and up to eight abreast in high density. Even a double lobe section was considered, space being available for the stowage of standard LD-1 and LD-3 containers under the main cabin floor.

For the long, thin routes with ranges of more than 9,262km, a four-engined 200-seater was studied; the four JT10D engines of 26,700lb thrust being shoulder-mounted for noise suppression. This engine configuration, however, suffered again from structural and aerodynamic complications, and by 1974 a return had been made to the simpler podded underwing engine installation, twin and three-engined variants still being considered.

In order to establish an overall need, between 30 and 40 airlines were contacted by Boeing, including the major US domestics and the European operators. United Airlines undertook to co-ordinate the data from the US airlines, remaining active in the overall 767 definition until the launch of the programme when it became the first customer. However, throughout the mid-1970s, no consensus could be found on which to establish a final design.

In concept the 7X7 was seen as a wide-body medium or long-range aircraft, the twin version having podded underwing engines, and the trijet with the third engine in the rear fuselage. The position of the tailplane alternated between low mounted on the fuselage and the T-type configuration. The wing would be a thick section, aft-loaded advanced supercritical design to maintain low drag and fuel efficiency. The variables still included the payload/range parameters, the cabin length and cross-section and the power plant.

At the Paris show in June 1975, Boeing showed, in conjunction with Aeritalia, a model of the 7X7 which featured a low tail and three engines. With the demise of so many other commercial airliner programmes, it was considered Boeing was not taking advantage of technology recycling by adapting existing airframes. In fact, Boeing was also doing this with the stretched 727-300 first revealed in early 1974. One of the major problems of launching a completely new airliner in a period of high inflation, is that the increasing cost becomes progressively more difficult to recover. At this time, Boeing was considering producing initially a medium range aircraft, which depending on adequate sales, would finance the development of a long-range version some two years behind. In order to overcome the inflationary headwind, the new project would need a combination of low-cost engineering techniques, including the use of composite materials and new aerodynamics, power plants and systems to increase efficiency, reducing fuel consumption and noise. Two fuselage lengths accommodating from 175 to 201 passengers, with an inclusive tour layout carrying up to 283 were on offer. Five power plant options were available and three range options of up to 4,000km for the European carriers, 5,000km for the US domestic trunks and over 9,000km for the intercontinental routes. Being roughly two thirds of the size of the wide-bodied trijets, the 7X7 would not be in competition, but complementary to them. At least the fuselage width had been set at 198 inches, allowing a twin-aisle seven-abreast layout.

Operating costs would be further reduced by installing an integrated digital system for flight control and navigation. This was to be combined with digitally generated cathode-ray tube (CRT) displays, reducing the cockpit workload to make it suitable for two crew operation.

By the 1980s a 6-7% growth was expected in worldwide air transport, together with a greater number of extended range non-stop routes. Combining this growth with noise and fuel efficiency demands, Boeing predicted a market for 1,500 aircraft, of which they expected to sell 1,000 7X7s over a period of 15 years, half to the US trunks, which were considered a major ingredient of any commercial success. A launch of the programme would be based on a largely common requirement from two major US airlines and one export sale, most likely from Europe. A four year development programme was planned with initial deliveries expected in late 1980 or early 1981, depending upon a suitable launch. Over a period of two years, Boeing had spent $40 million and the Italian government had invested $230 million in a production facility for 7X7 components. With a 20% share, Aeritalia was a risk sharing partner, building and testing hardware and working on detailed aerodynamics. Nearly 400 engineers, including Aeritalia personnel, were working on the programme.

In June 1976 the concept had been further refined to a low tailed twin 7X7-962 with very high aspect ratio wings and the double-lobe

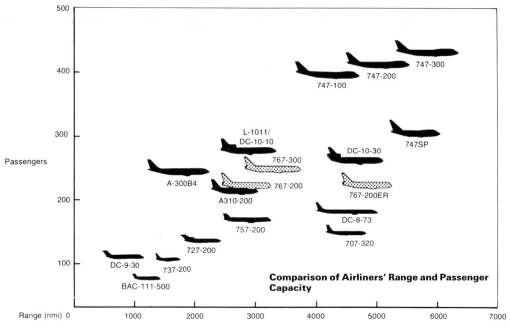

Comparison of Airliners' Range and Passenger Capacity

Chart axes — Passengers (vertical, 100 to 500), Range (nmi) (horizontal, 0 to 7000)

Aircraft plotted: 747-300, 747-200, 747-100, 747SP, L-1011/DC-10-10, DC-10-30, 767-300, 767-200, 767-200ER, A-300B4, A310-200, 757-200, DC-8-73, 707-320, 727-200, DC-9-30, 737-200, BAC-111-500

fuselage diameter increased to 210in permitting up to eight abreast seating for 200 passengers in a twin-aisle layout, 20 first-class and 180 tourist-class, over stage lengths of up to 2,700 miles. A competing 7X7-963 trijet was being studied by a completely different team of designers, the twin being favoured for maintenance costs, but requiring greater installed power to overcome the engine failure case. Composite materials were to be used in the manufacture of floor panels, wing leading edges, inboard ailerons, elevators, centre engine duct of the trijet, parts of the flaps and a range of other components including non-structural fairings. Other structural advances would include stringerless sidewalls, titanium centre-section and carbon brakes. Every 100lb of weight saved was estimated to be worth 50nm additional range with a given payload.

The use of digital computers in the flight control system, the heading and altitude reference systems and air data computers gave reduced weight, cutting maintenance with higher reliability and improved performance. An electronic auto throttle control could be used throughout the flight to maintain best economy.

Between mid 1976 and the spring of 1977 further major configuration changes were made, both the 7X7 and the smaller 7N7 adopting T-tails again. In this form they were shown for the first time at the Paris Air Show in June 1977. The 7X7 twin had been deleted from the range and the trijet had only 20 more passenger seats over the narrow-body 7N7. The major differences were range, freight capacity and over-water capability.

Still no firm decision for launch could be made, the go-ahead having been hoped for in October 1977. Prospective US launch airlines could still not agree on fuselage width and number of engines. To find a compromise, Boeing reverted later in the year to a 198in wide fuselage, and its twin-jet first, followed later by trijet philosophy, which was a step back to earlier proposals.

On 5 January 1978 Boeing confirmed its dedication to the new commercial airliner programme by announcing plans to extend its plant at Everett, which had been originally built 10 years earlier to produce the 747. In the middle of the following month, Boeing allotted the designations 757, 767 and 777 to a range of new and derivative airliner projects. Instructions were given to progress towards starting a new aircraft programme, with firm specifications allowing sales efforts to start in earnest with the aim of launch orders and go-ahead around mid-1978.

The new Boeing designations were for a 757 narrow-body twin-jet derived from the 727-300, and seating 150-170 passengers; the 767-100 all new semi-wide body (198in) seven-abreast twin-jet fitting the American Airlines requirement of flying 175 passengers over a 2,000nm stage length; the 767-200 offering the same range, but with two more seat rows for the United requirement of 190 passengers; the 777-100, a trijet version of the 767 with a transcontinental range of about 2,700nm carrying 175 passengers; and the 777-200 with an 'oceanic' range of 4,500nm, a little less than the 5,000nm plus of the big jets.

The wings, flightdeck, body section and tail components were common to all members of the 767/777 family. A go ahead for both the 757 and 767/777 programmes was desirable by the end of 1978, but the company was reluctant to increase manpower enough to take on both programmes unaided. A way to overcome this was international collaboration; the Aeritalia agreement on participation on the 7X7 project being transferred to the 767/777 programme, with Japanese co-operation also being sought. The choice of engines was still as open as ever.

The 767 was now coming out as a shorter range aircraft, but with the common wing policy was somewhat over-winged, to cope with the higher gross weights of the long-range 777. However, this did allow a much simpler range of high lift devices on both the leading and trailing edges of the wings.

In May 1978 the 767 appeared to be gaining favour, with the -200 given priority because of a choice of three proven engines and a firm interest by United Airlines. Certification and initial deliveries were expected in mid-1982. Design work was progressing on wing engineering, over 67 different wind tunnel models having been tested. The overall area was nearly 2,900sq ft, bigger than the rival Airbus competition. The 777 trijet was still planned to follow after about nine months, to give time for the development of the cropped fan power plants, the main interest coming from American Airlines for their long-range intercontinental routes.

The seven-abreast layout was preferred as it catered most effectively with 150-250 seats without being structurally too long or aerodynamically too short. Although this allowed twin-aisle operation in the passenger cabin, the underfloor cargo hold could take only one LD-3 standard container, not two across as in the Airbus, and Boeing, therefore, proposed LD-3A containers produced specially for the 767/777 family of airliners.

The new aircraft would be produced at the expanding Everett facility, bringing combined output with the 747 to 200 aircraft annually, employing nearly 12,000 people over a seven year build up. The 767/777 production rate would preferably start at around two per month for the first couple of years. The market was seen as 1,500 767s and 777-100s worth $32,000 million, plus 300-400 777-200s worth $10,000 million. Competition was keen but the efficiency of the new aircraft would fend off the smaller types, and the big jets were an overkill of capacity on some thin routes. The total investment in the 767/777 programme could reach $1,500 million by 1986, largely financed from its own resources, but with hoped-for support from Italy and Japan.

On 14 July 1978 came the long awaited airline decision, when United Airlines place an order for 30 767-200 aircraft for service entry in mid-1982. It had been a closely fought competition for the Airbus A310, but United made their decision six weeks earlier than expected for a 198in wide seven-abreast accommodating 197 passengers in a twin-lobe fuselage aircraft with a low-set tailplane. Power was to come from a pair of Pratt & Whitney JT9D-7R engines developing 44,300lb thrust, a derated and modified version of the engines used in United's Boeing 747s. Total value of the 767s, plus spares, simulators and training, was worth around $1,200 million. The biggest change to the design, literally weeks before the signing of the order, was the change from T-tail to fuselage mounted. The range was 2,200 miles to cover United's critical transcontinental routes from Denver to the East Coast and Cleveland to the West Coast. Further refinement of the aircraft was under way during the detailed design stage, amongst which was the modification of the fuselage section to allow 22 LD-2 containers in the underfloor hold, plus additional room for bulk cargo. Meanwhile the trijet 777 was quietly shelved, any extended range developments being looked after by developing the basic 767 airframe.

Right:
The Boeing 777 tri-jet long-range fan-jet airliner project was dropped in favour of long range developments of the 767.

2. Boeing 757 Conception

During the mid-1970s, in order to overcome the inflationary spiral associated with the development of a totally new airliner, Boeing was investigating the stretching of their well proven 727 and 737 airframes. At the Paris Air Show in June 1975 a model of the 727-300 was shown, having been revealed originally in early 1974. In addition to the minimum change 727-300A, the -300B had a stretched fuselage to accommodate up to 189 passengers, its three 20,000lb-thrust JT8D-217 engines taking it over stage lengths of 2,000nm. United Airlines had shown interest in the slightly more advanced 727-300B, but continued to postpone its decision on ordering, a major disadvantage being the need for quieter and more efficient fan engines.

Above:
British Airways shared the launch of the Boeing 757 with Eastern Airlines when their combined orders for 40 aircraft were announced on 31 August 1978.

A year later the smaller capacity narrow bodied aircraft had gained the designation 7N7 having a 40-50% commonality with the 737 airframe. The major changes included in the project, given the Boeing design number 761, were a completely new advanced technology wing attached to a stretched fuselage which could have the option of a two or three crew flightdeck. Power was to come from a pair of wing-mounted podded CFM56 or JT10D engines. Two fuselage lengths were offered, either accommodating 154 or 169 passengers, and still air range was in excess of 2,000nm.

In mid-1977 the 7N7 appeared as a largely new airframe featuring a T-tail and two wing-mounted engines. Smaller members of the narrow-bodied family had been abandoned, bringing the 7N7 within a 20-seat capacity of the 7X7. Since the rejection of the 727-300B project by United, the 7N7 was aimed at this still-to-be-satisfied requirement. Seating capacities ranged from 160 to 180 passengers and proposed powerplants could be Pratt & Whitney JT10D-4s or cropped fan RB211-535s or CF6-32s.

The 7N7 economy depended on low structural weight, little more than the 727-200, despite the increased capacity. Its range was planned around a one-stop coast-to-coast US operation. This relatively short 700nm-sector helped to keep down both weight and costs. The generous wing area would, however, allow room for additional fuel to cater for the longer European sectors, and hot and high operations.

The T-tail layout was chosen virtually by accident. When the basic 727 empennage, without the centre engine duct, was wind tunnel tested, it was found to save two percent of the fuel consumption, without any additional weight or superstall problems. Developments of both the 737 and 727 had not, however, been abandoned.

By August 1977 the 7N7 had been radically remodelled, bringing its cabin cross-section to a similar size to the 7X7. The six-abreast cross-section of the earlier Boeings was discarded for the seven-abreast twin-aisle layout. In this form, it was Boeing's leading contender for the US domestic market. Having grown from a 120-seater, it was now being offered in 160 and 180 passenger versions to US domestic standards. Power was to be from a pair of wing-mounted cropped-fan engines. The change in fuselage cross-section was brought about by the airline customers, particularly United, reacting against the narrow-bodied 1950s six-abreast fuselage sections, partly because of a wish to improve passenger comfort, and also because it could prove difficult to stretch a long thin fuselage beyond a 180-seat capacity. The initial Boeing response to the passenger comfort was to increase the width of the narrow fuselage by six inches, but the wider twin-aisle fuselage was seen to give more development potential.

This bigger 7N7 was a close challenge to the 7X7 in the market place, and was more of a completely new aircraft than the earlier derivative studies. This would involve a much higher design and engineering effort by Boeing, the investment in time and money delaying the launch of the 7X7. The go ahead for the seven-abreast 7N7 could well push the 7X7 a long way into the future.

Below:
Icelandair's first Boeing 757-200 was delivered in 1990. The arrival of the Boeing 757s on the carrier's trans-Atlantic routes concluded a two-year renewal programme of all Icelandair's international craft.

There was, however, a lack of airline enthusiasm for the seven-abreast seating, which added one line of seats at the expense of an extra aisle, and offered no great passenger appeal over the eight-abreast layout of the Airbus A300. It was also unable to accept a pair of LD-3 standard containers in the underfloor hold, as were other wide-bodied jets.

In February 1978 the 7N7 became the Boeing 757, returning to the narrow-body configuration, but still as a twin-jet powered by under-slung cropped-fan engines such as the General Electric CF6-32 or Rolls-Royce RB211-535s. Uprated Pratt & Whitney JT8D-209s or a JT10D derivative could also be used. The 757 used the 727 fuselage cross-section, flightdeck and modified empennage, but fitted with a new wing. The 150-170 seating capacity, depending on arrangement, corresponded closely to the 727-300B project abandoned in 1975. British Aerospace had been offered design and manufacture of the wing, a move welcomed by the British Government, as it was seen as a breakthrough into the large US domestic and world markets. British Aerospace was, however, very much aware of the advantages of being part of a strong European aircraft industry, the Boeing talks being little more than investigatory.

It was in fact British Airways and Eastern Airlines, who as main potential initial customers for the 757, helped Boeing draft a joint specification for the aircraft. The proposed 150-seater was stretched by two seat rows to accommodate 162 passengers for Eastern, and for British Airways around 175. The unit price of the aircraft was increased from $14.3 million to $14.75 million for the larger version. The 757 was seen to have range and payload advantages over the less costly, but competitive DC-9-80, and at least one establish DC-9 operator was showing serious interest in the 757. The US local airlines were seen as the main initial market for the aircraft, providing the DC-9 variants did not gain too great a foothold.

The airframe was still old technology based on the 727/737 to keep the costs down, but the airlines could be prepared to pay up to a further $2 million per aircraft to make them technically more acceptable with the latest design standards. A further three seat row stretch 757-200 would give 180 seats, making the passenger capacity the same as the 767-100, although significantly smaller than the 767-200. Even using new technology, the 757-200 at $18 million

would be cheaper to buy than the $22.5 million 767-100 and the seat/mile costs would be considerably less than with any comparable wide-bodied airliner.

With deregulation in the USA bringing down fares and reducing yields, the cost of flying another aisle around the sky would not be very attractive. Lower fares could expand the 757 market and might lead to eventual traffic growth and a demand for larger aircraft.

The 757 was offered with the Rolls-Royce RB211-535 as the favoured lead engine, with the CF6-32 or JT10D as options. With the Rolls-Royce engine the gross weight was expected to be 192,200lb with fuel burn per passenger of 56lb over a 500nm stage. Fuel consumption was typically 15% better than the 727 and fuel burn per passenger 30% better. Take off distance of the 757 was planned for around 6,000ft, 1,000ft less than the 727. The 757, with its four-wheel bogie main undercarriage, would have a load classification number (LCN) of under 50, allowing it to operate without restriction from difficult airports such as LaGuardia in New York. The approach speed of 125kt gives a wet runway landing distance of less than 5,000ft. Having experienced lack of wing area in the 727 and 737, Boeing has given the 757 a large wing of 1,950sq ft area to avoid future development problems.

By May 1979 Boeing was committed to the launch of both the 757 and 767, defining the specifications to allow finite discussions with the prospective launch customers. This dual launch effort involved a considerable investment effort by Boeing, both in finance and resources. The decision on the cabin width had not been an easy one. A narrow body looks good in the

certification, to the pilots being cleared to fly both types of aircraft without conversion from one to the other. As well as the flightdeck equipment, the auxiliary power units, electrical power generation and air-conditioning equipment were common to both aircraft.

Although the physically smaller of the two programmes, the 757 was still a big project. It was only about two feet longer than the 727-200, but it had an extra 26.8ft of cabin length, in a fuselage which could be lengthened or shortened. Originally the aircraft had been proposed with an adapted 727 T-tail, but as the overall dimensions increased, the commonality advantage faded, the low-set layout being adopted, sharing where practical many components with the 767. The wings were to have a sweepback of about 25° at quarter-chord with double-slotted trailing edge flaps and full span leading edge slats to give good airfield characteristics.

First flight of the 757 was due from Renton, where the flight development programme would take place, in February 1982. Up to five aircraft would be used in the programme over a seven month period, totalling some 1,250 flying hours for an in-service date of January 1983 with the Rolls-Royce engines. If a customer were to specify the 35,580lb-thrust GE CF6-32, deliveries would be around August 1983. Boeing was also planning to build up substantial production rates ahead of airline deliveries, aiming to reach four or five a month, with 19 aircraft completed in time for certification.

At the Paris Show in June 1979 Boeing showed for the first time models of the 757 with the new nose shape incorporating the flight deck of the 767. British Airways added 18 options to their firm order for 19 aircraft, all fitted with the new advanced technology flightdeck. Having started out as a derivative of the Boeing 727, the 757 now shared only the fuselage cross-section with the earlier type. Two versions of the 757 were offered, both with Rolls-Royce engines, but with the option of GE power, one with a gross weight of 220,000lb, carrying typically 196 passengers in a one-class 34in pitch over a range of 2,000 miles, or a gross weight of 230,000lb over a 2,500nm range.

Although the decision to redefine the 757 as an aircraft with comparable technology to the 767 increased development costs, savings were made in production, particularly the doubling up of orders on common equipment to give keener prices.

smaller capacities, but does not stretch well. A wide-body, however, becomes too dumpy at the lower end of the scale.

The 757 was effectively launched by a simultaneous commitment for 40 aircraft in August 1978: 19 for British Airways and 21 for Eastern Airlines. Boeing only confirmed their go-ahead in March 1979. Both airlines chose the Rolls-Royce RB211-535 engines which gave a suitable power source to ensure a first flight for late 1981.

The launch gap between the two programmes ensured a more even distribution of funds, the 757 and 767 being split between two different design teams in two manufacturing locations. The 757 was allocated to the existing narrow-bodied airliner plant at Renton where the 707/727/737 were developed. The design team proposed the same fuselage cross section as the earlier airliners, relying on wing technology derived partly from the 767 development, but with more complex trailing edge flaps. The 757 was seen as a smaller and lower risk project, but certainly not second best. Economics obviously played a key part in the programme and the excellent seat/mile costs of the 757 had a major influence. Also to save costs, both the 757 and 767 were to have some identical systems, particularly on the flightdeck and avionics equipment. As a result the vee-shaped windscreen used on the 727 was abandoned for the 757 and the curved windscreen was adopted, the 757 requiring a new tapered forward fuselage section between the flightdeck and parallel fuselage section. This reduced overall length slightly, but increased passenger accommodation by three seats. This gave the 757 a somewhat unusual nose shape, but it did allow commonality of flightdeck layout, which eventually led, following

3. The 767 Design and Development

In structural terms, the Boeing 767 is traditional, but major advances have been made with materials, new aluminium alloys being used which offer better strength and corrosion resistance than previously. Computer aided design (CAD) was used extensively, providing the design parameters to the production tooling for cost effective manufacture. The use of composite materials in a number of secondary structural components represented a weight saving of some 1,000lb over the use of light alloys for the same items. The principal composite material is the du Pont Kevlar graphite/epoxy, which is used in the manufacture of such items as the ailerons, elevators, rudder, spoilers, the wing to fuselage fairings, undercarriage doors, the fixed wing leading and trailing edge panels and engine cowling skins. Nomex honeycomb panels are used in some areas, examples being the cabin floor panels.

One of the longest lead items on any aircraft is the undercarriage units. The nose undercarriage has a twin-wheel steerable unit controlled by both pilots, while the two main undercarriage units carry a typical Boeing four-wheel bogie, which retracts inwards to lie in the fuselage between the forward and rear freight holds. The massive load-carrying shock struts for the main legs are one-piece forgings in vacuum-melted steel, orders being placed for suitable forgings some months before launch of the aircraft, to reduce the risk of any delays. The undercarriage is hydraulically operated, locked in the up position by the gear doors, and in an emergency can be lowered by gravity.

The 767 takes full advantage of the latest developments in supercritical wing technology and with its aft-loaded section develops more lift for less drag than earlier jets, being the key to the aircraft efficiency. The wing section is some 22% thicker than that in use a decade earlier, allowing a lighter, simpler structure with more capacity for fuel, giving greater range. Control is by a complex range of devices on the wing comprising outboard low-speed ailerons; inboard high-speed ailerons which droop in unison with the flaps to reduce the nose up angle of attack for better view on the approach; flight and ground spoilers which are electrically commanded, whereas the other controls are conventional; and leading and trailing-edge flaps. The leading-edge flaps, or slats, are in six sections on each wing and can be set in various positions in relation to the trailing edge flaps for optimum

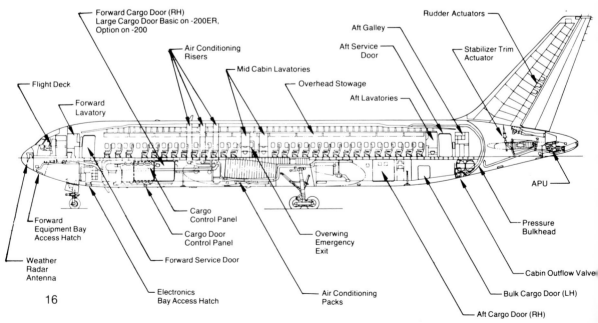

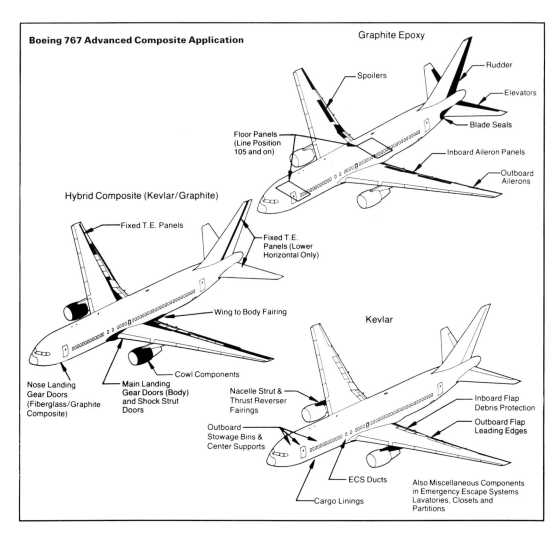

Boeing 767 Advanced Composite Application

Graphite Epoxy

- Spoilers
- Rudder
- Elevators
- Blade Seals
- Inboard Aileron Panels
- Outboard Ailerons
- Floor Panels (Line Position 105 and on)

Hybrid Composite (Kevlar/Graphite)

- Fixed T.E. Panels
- Fixed T.E. Panels (Lower Horizontal Only)
- Wing to Body Fairing
- Cowl Components
- Nose Landing Gear Doors (Fiberglass/Graphite Composite)
- Main Landing Gear Doors (Body) and Shock Strut Doors

Kevlar

- Nacelle Strut & Thrust Reverser Fairings
- Outboard Stowage Bins & Center Supports
- Inboard Flap Debris Protection
- Outboard Flap Leading Edges
- ECS Ducts
- Cargo Linings
- Also Miscellaneous Components in Emergency Escape Systems Lavatories, Closets and Partitions

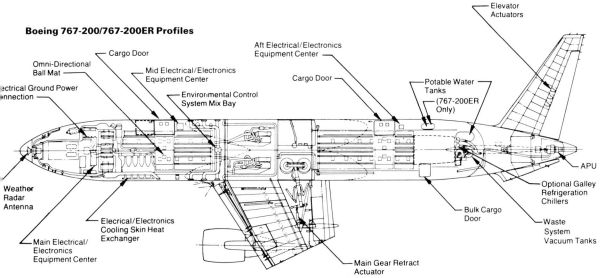

Boeing 767-200/767-200ER Profiles

- Elevator Actuators
- Cargo Door
- Omni-Directional Ball Mat
- Aft Electrical/Electronics Equipment Center
- Mid Electrical/Electronics Equipment Center
- Cargo Door
- Electrical Ground Power Connection
- Environmental Control System Mix Bay
- Potable Water Tanks (767-200ER Only)
- Weather Radar Antenna
- APU
- Optional Galley Refrigeration Chillers
- Elecrical/Electronics Cooling Skin Heat Exchanger
- Bulk Cargo Door
- Waste System Vacuum Tanks
- Main Electrical/ Electronics Equipment Center
- Main Gear Retract Actuator

17

Boeing 767 Control Actuation

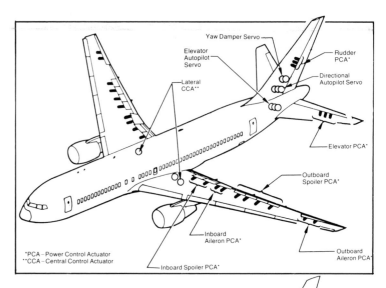

*PCA – Power Control Actuator
**CCA – Central Control Actuator

Boeing 767 High Lift Devices

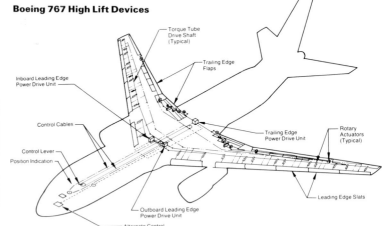

Trailing Edge Flaps

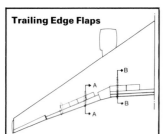

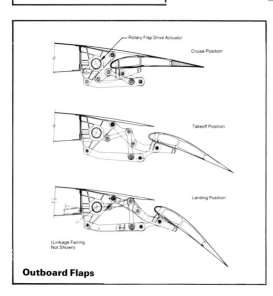

Outboard Flaps

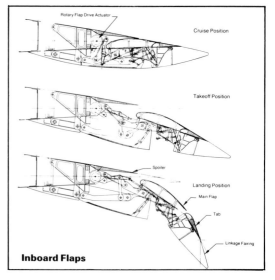

Inboard Flaps

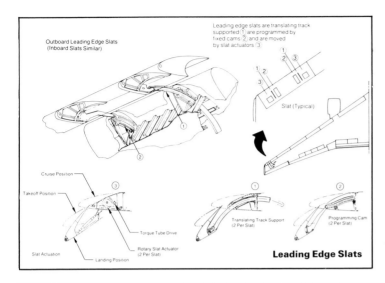

Outboard Leading Edge Slats
(Inboard Slats Similar)

Leading edge slats are translating track supported (1) are programmed by fixed cams (2) and are moved by slat actuators (3)

Slat (Typical)

Cruise Position
Takeoff Position
Slat Actuation
Landing Position
Torque Tube Drive
Rotary Slat Actuator (2 Per Slat)

Translating Track Support (2 Per Slat)

Programming Cam (2 Per Slat)

Leading Edge Slats

Below:
The first Boeing 767, N767BA, was retained by the company for continuing development work.

performance during take-off and landing. The single slotted flaps cover the whole wing trailing-edge not occupied by the ailerons. A conventional rudder and elevators are fitted to the swept-back tail surfaces.

Boeing undertook a large amount of wind tunnel testing on the 767 to develop and prove its shape. Well over 26,000hr of wind tunnel work was accumulated, which compared with 14,000hr for the 747 and a mere 4,000hr for the 727.

As with any airliner, structural testing of components and airframe is a major part of certification. Boeing prepared one complete airframe for static testing in three phases. The first was to test the 767's ability to carry normal design loads, phase two subjected the airframe to loads representative of growth development, and the final phase was a composite of worst design cases resulting in the destruction of the specimen. Slats and flaps were also tested to destruction and the undercarriage back-up structure

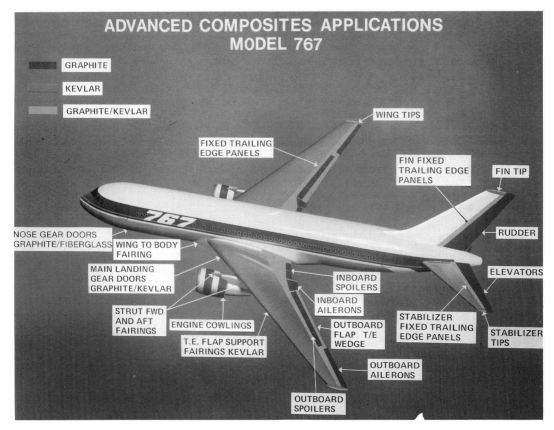

ADVANCED COMPOSITES APPLICATIONS
MODEL 767

GRAPHITE

KEVLAR

GRAPHITE/KEVLAR

WING TIPS

FIXED TRAILING
EDGE PANELS

FIN FIXED
TRAILING EDGE
PANELS

FIN TIP

NOSE GEAR DOORS
GRAPHITE/FIBERGLASS

WING TO BODY
FAIRING

RUDDER

MAIN LANDING
GEAR DOORS
GRAPHITE/KEVLAR

INBOARD
SPOILERS

ELEVATORS

INBOARD
AILERONS

STRUT FWD
AND AFT
FAIRINGS

ENGINE COWLINGS

OUTBOARD
FLAP T/E
WEDGE

STABILIZER
FIXED TRAILING
EDGE PANELS

STABILIZER
TIPS

T.E. FLAP SUPPORT
FAIRINGS KEVLAR

OUTBOARD
AILERONS

OUTBOARD
SPOILERS

surveyed. Beginning in April 1982 fatigue testing concentrated on one fairly complete airframe consisting of wing, fuselage and fin, and was also supported by component trials, the aim being to complete 25,000 cycles by certification, to keep well ahead of actual flying operations. By March 1983 the static test airframe had reached the equivalent of 20 years flying. Fatigue testing by the same time had duplicated 50,000 flights. Following 18 months of airframe testing, by November 1983, the structural design using new processes and materials for the first time in a contemporary airliner had been proven. The test airframe had completed 100,000 flight cycles, equivalent to 40 years of airline service, in a series of fatigue tests at Boeing's Everett plant. The structural modifications required for this programme were found to be insignificant, considering the airframe had completed two full-service life cycles.

Primary power for the aircraft controls and undercarriage is provided by three independent hydraulic systems, two of which are operated by engine-driven pumps plus electric pumps, while the third is powered by two electric pumps and an air-driven pump running off the auxiliary power unit (APU). Emergency power for the pri-

Above:
Advanced composites were used extensively in the construction of non-primary structural components of the 767.

mary flight controls, flaps and slats, tailplane incidence trim, landing gear operation, nose-wheel steering and wheel brakes is provided by two transformer rectifiers and a nickel cadmium battery.

The 767 was designed from the start to be operated by a two-man crew, although initial certification was with a three-man layout in case of union manning problems and safety aspects. The roomy flightdeck has been designed to the latest comfort and efficiency standards using the most advanced ideas in information displays and digital technology. Both pilots are provided with three cathode ray tube (CRT) displays replacing many of the traditional analogue instruments. One CRT is for the primary flight instruments, replacing the altitude-indicator; another for the horizontal situation indication, on which can also be selected weather radar or compass display; and the third providing a central caution and warning system. With these displays, the crew workload is reduced, with only the information required for any phase of the flight being presented. This includes the checklists, each item of which has to be actioned, before acceptance of the next item. The Sperry digital automatic flight management system (FMS) allows automatic landings to full Cat IIIB standard. The FMS offers far more than the usual area-navigation and performance data computer fitted to the previous generation airliners, and allows the crew to achieve a more economical utilisation. It has a dual-CRT display panel and keyboard mounted on the centre panel, forward of the throttles. Above this panel is the central warning CRT, the urgency of any warnings being indicated by red for urgent, amber for precautionary and green for information. They are accompanied by flashing lights, the information on the flat screens being clear enough to be seen in the brightest sunlight.

The 767 is very much a risk-sharing programme with subcontractors involved more heavily than previous aircraft such as the 747. Boeing planned to manufacture 53% by value of the first 200 aircraft, consisting of the wing, engine nacelles, nose section and cabin floor. Major international risk sharing partners are the Japanese Commercial Transport Development Corporation (CTDC) and Aeritalia of Italy. Over

100 staff from each organisation were trained and briefed by Boeing before returning to their companies to supervise detailed design and manufacture. CTDC is a consortium of Fuji, Kawasaki and Mitsubishi, with a responsibility for fuselage panels, doors, wing to fuselage fairings, main undercarriage doors and between spar wing ribs. Kawasaki is also responsible for wing flap gearboxes and Teijin Seiki for the wing spoiler actuators, both as subcontractors. Aeritalia has responsibility for wing control surfaces, including trailing-edge flaps and leading-edge slats, wing tips, elevators, rudder and radome. The remaining 767 major suppliers are North American based.

As an example of Italian involvement in the 767, over $94 million had been invested in the programme by the time the aircraft was in flight development. A substantial share of technology, mainly in the form of advanced composite structures was of Italian design and manufacture. These structures cover some 30% of the aircraft's external surface area and include the largest carbon fibre components yet produced for a commercial aircraft. This was Aeritalia's first involvement in a commercial risk-sharing venture and it helped to regenerate the industry by providing an impetus for an accelerated upgrading of the technological capability. Boeing's stringent specifications taught new disciplines, by introducing advanced materials and new design

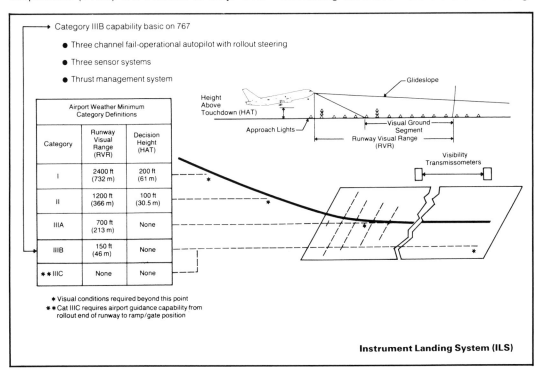

Instrument Landing System (ILS)

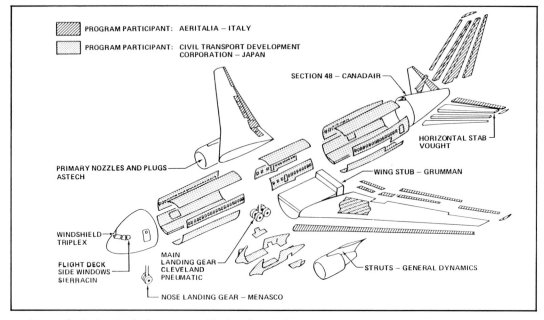

PROGRAM PARTICIPANT: AERITALIA – ITALY

PROGRAM PARTICIPANT: CIVIL TRANSPORT DEVELOPMENT CORPORATION – JAPAN

SECTION 48 – CANADAIR

HORIZONTAL STAB VOUGHT

PRIMARY NOZZLES AND PLUGS ASTECH

WING STUB – GRUMMAN

WINDSHIELD TRIPLEX

MAIN LANDING GEAR CLEVELAND PNEUMATIC

FLIGHT DECK SIDE WINDOWS SIERRACIN

STRUTS – GENERAL DYNAMICS

NOSE LANDING GEAR – MENASCO

and manufacturing techniques, provided a firm foundation for a fundamental diversification programme.

At the programme launch, Aeritalia had anticipated producing 8·5 sets per month for Boeing by the time the aircraft was in service. Each set, valued in 1982 levels at $1.2 million, represented 12.5% of the total value of the airframe. In fact, when Aeritalia signed the contract to become a major risk-sharing partner in the 767 develop-

Above:
Boeing 767 Programme Participation and Major Structural Sub-Contracts.

Below:
Although the 767 is assembled at Everett, the manufacture of the major components is shared widely from as far away as Italy and Japan.

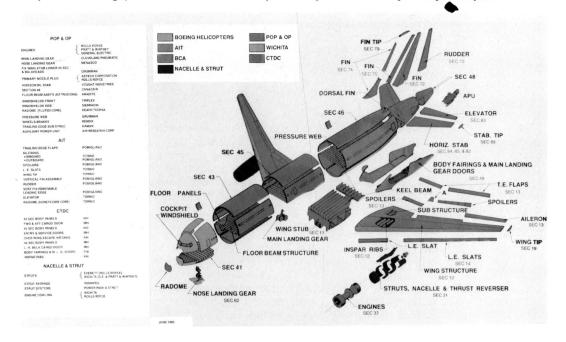

POP & OP	
ENGINES	ROLLS ROYCE / PRATT & WHITNEY / GENERAL ELECTRIC
MAIN LANDING GEAR	CLEVELAND PNEUMATIC
NOSE LANDING GEAR	MENASCO
FIX WING STUB LOWER 45 SEC & BULKHEADS	GRUMMAN
PRIMARY NOZZLE PLUG	ASTECH CORPORATION / ROLLS ROYCE
HORIZONTAL STAB	VOUGHT INDUSTRIES
SECTION 48	CANADAIR
FLOOR BEAM ASSYS (EXTRUSIONS)	ANADITE
WINDSHIELDS FRONT	TRIPLEX
WINDSHIELDS SIDE	SIERRACIN
RADOME (FLUTED CORE)	HEATH-TECHNA
PRESSURE WEB	GRUMMAN
WHEELS/BRAKES	BENDIX
TRAILING EDGE SUB-STRUC	KAMAN
AUXILIARY POWER UNIT	AIR RESEARCH CORP

AIT	
TRAILING EDGE FLAPS	POMIGLIANO
AILERONS	
• INBOARD	TORINO
• OUTBOARD	POMIGLIANO
SPOILERS	POMIGLIANO
L. E. SLATS	TORINO
WING TIP	TORINO
VERTICAL FIN ASSEMBLY	POMIGLIANO
RUDDER	POMIGLIANO
VERT FIN REMOVABLE LEADING EDGE	POMIGLIANO
ELEVATOR	TORINO
RADOME (HONEYCOMB CORE)	TORINO

CTDC	
45 SEC BODY PANELS	KHI
FWD & AFT CARGO DOOR	MHI
45 SEC BODY PANELS	KHI
ENTRY & SERVICE DOORS	MHI
OVER WING ESCAPE HATCHES	KHI
46 SEC BODY PANELS	MHI
L. H. BULK CARGO DOOR	MHI
BODY FAIRINGS & M. L. G. DOORS	FHI
INSPAR RIBS	FHI

NACELLE & STRUT	
STRUTS	EVERETT (ROLLS ROYCE) / WICHITA (G.E. & PRATT & WHITNEY)
STRUT FAIRINGS	WINNIPEG
STRUT SYSTEMS	POWER PACK & STRUT
ENGINE COWLING	WICHITA / ROLLS ROYCE

BOEING HELICOPTERS
AIT
BCA
NACELLE & STRUT
POP & OP
WICHITA
CTDC

FIN TIP SEC 79
RUDDER SEC 73
FIN SEC 74
FIN SEC 75
FIN SEC 72
SEC 48
DORSAL FIN
APU
SEC 46
ELEVATOR SEC 83
PRESSURE WEB
STAB. TIP SEC 89
HORIZ. STAB SEC 84, 85, & 82
SEC 45
BODY FAIRINGS & MAIN LANDING GEAR DOORS SEC 49
SEC 43
T.E. FLAPS SEC 13
FLOOR PANELS
KEEL BEAM A
SPOILERS
COCKPIT WINDSHIELD
SPOILERS SEC 13
SUB STRUCTURE
AILERON SEC 13
WING STUB SEC 11
MAIN LANDING GEAR
WING TIP SEC 19
FLOOR BEAM STRUCTURE
INSPAR RIBS SEC 12
L.E. SLAT
L.E. SLATS SEC 14
SEC 41
WING STRUCTURE SEC 12
RADOME
NOSE LANDING GEAR SEC 62
STRUTS, NACELLE & THRUST REVERSER SEC 31
ENGINES SEC 33

JUNE 1989

ment and production programme on 14 August 1978, it was committed to establishing a capacity to cater for peak outputs of up to 12.5 ship sets per month. The breakeven was anticipated on the delivery of the 501st set of assemblies.

However, in the early 1980s the airline industry was experiencing a lean period with the consequent sluggish market for new equipment. The initial production plans therefore had to be scaled down, an improvement in the situation being expected by the middle of the decade. The early optimism generated by an excellent initial order was hard to sustain during the following inactivity, including deferrals of deliveries and cancellation threats. Confidence in the eventual success, together with prospects for the long-haul developments never faltered.

The first 767, N767BA, was rolled out of the Everett production line on 4 August 1981 into the Pacific Coast sunshine in front of a large audience of Boeing workers, customer airline representatives and press. Work then commenced on preparation for the maiden flight, including fuel tank calibration, while final detail work was completed.

From the maiden flight of the first 767 on 26 September 1981 a highly demanding and intensive flight development programme commenced, the basic certification trials involving six

aircraft. The Boeing-owned first 767, powered by two Pratt & Whitney JT9D-7R4s under the command of Project test pilot, Tom Edmonds, rotated and climbed away from the Paine Field runway on its maiden flight three days earlier than scheduled three years before. The take-off run used a mere 3,000ft of the runway and the 2hr 4min sortie was judged a perfect flight, the aircraft behaving exactly as it was designed to do. With a gross weight of 240,000lb the crew checked the handling characteristics from the stall buffet speed of 102kt to 225kt. Flap operation was tested to the 30° down setting for landing, and the landing gear and speed brake operation were evaluated with flaps up and down. Particular praise was forthcoming for the digital flight instruments and CRTs for clarity and the ability to provide continuous, precise orientation.

Following the early tests, the first 767 was flown to the Boeing Development Centre between Renton and Seattle. The first aircraft was allocated to air worthiness, control, stability and aerodynamic performance. Flutter testing was completed in about 15hr of flying, and the aircraft reached Mach 0.91 and 43,100ft. Early flight trials covered longitudinal stability and control, buffet boundaries, dynamic damping and stall approach. During early December, the first aircraft was based at Palmdale, California, where the accessibility of the long runways at Edward's Air Force Base allowed adequate room for minimum unstick velocity trials and other tests. The second aircraft, which first flew on 4 November, tested controls, digital avionics, engines and electrics. The third 767 surveyed flight loads,

Above:
The major 767 development was the series 300 with a fuselage stretch of 21ft 1in/6.43m, increasing the seating capacity by 50 passengers.

examined stall and buffet characteristics, and tested pneumatics and automatic flight controls. The fourth aircraft investigated noise and aerodynamic measurements, the fifth covering performance with the GE engine as specified by Delta. Each 767 was expected to fly about 30hr testing per month with a total of 1,100-1,300hr planned, although this increased to 1,600hr. The certification programme was completed in a mere 10 months, meeting a date set by the manufacturer as far back as December 1978. This date of 30 July 1982 was met despite an additional 185hr of certification flying caused by the fundamental change from a three to two-crew operation part way through the programme. This achievement was even more remarkable due to the fact that for half the time that the 767 certification was under way, Boeing was engaged in parallel flight testing of the 757.

The first aircraft VA001 is Boeing owned, and will be retained by them, but subsequent aircraft in the test programme were destined for delivery to either United or Delta. The second aircraft VA002 was used for FAA test participation, commencing on 10 December 1981, joined in the test programme by VA003 on 28 December and VA004 two days later. All three of these production aircraft were part of the United order and were powered by the Pratt & Whitney JT9D-7R4 engines, and the similarly powered VA001 joined the certification programme in February 1982. Of the first 17 customer airlines announced, 10 selected this engine, with the remainder specifying the GE CF6-80A.

The first four aircraft flew a total of 1,445 flying hours in 1,251 sorties up to the end of June 1982, to which was added 239 hours in 230

flights by the CF6-80A-powered VA301 which joined the test fleet on 19 February 1982. VA301 commenced its certification flying in March with full clearance for commercial operations after six months.

One of the major challenges of the 767 test programme, which was handled by the second and third aircraft, was the checking out of the new avionics. These included the digital flight control systems, mostly integrated with digital driven CRT displays, the completely new laser-gyro inertial reference system, the pitch augmentation control system (PACS) and the auto-throttle systems. This was amongst the many reasons why the test programme called for five fully-equipped test aircraft, each carrying 30,000lb of test equipment, including 4,000lb of wiring in the wings alone.

The Boeing 767 VA006 N605UA was the first to fly in the two-crew configuration and completed a demanding 15-day seven-country demonstration tour of Europe and the Middle East, combining sales presentations in the Airbus stronghold with the FAA monitored functional and reliability (F&R) testing, equivalent to route proving flights. During the tour a total of nearly 81hr were flown on 43 flights, carrying more than thirteen hundred officials from governments, airlines and industry, as well as press.

The aircraft used on this international tour was the seventh aircraft off the assembly line and the fifth aircraft for United Airlines, the launch cus-

tomer. Following the favourable findings of a US presidential task force regarding the safety of two-crew airliner operation, 16 of Boeing's initial 17 customers switched to a two-crew flightdeck. VA006 was therefore immediately moved to the modification shop after its roll-out from the final assembly bay at Everett on 16 January 1982 to have its three-crew flightdeck modified to a two-crew configuration. With modifications complete, it entered the test programme on 27 May and accumulated some 60hr by 6 July when it left Seattle for its 29,000 mile tour. Amongst the occupants were three Boeing pilots, three FAA pilots, a number of FAA staff responsible for the monitoring of F&R testing, a 19-man Boeing maintenance crew and a number of officials from Boeing and Aeritalia. A fuelling stop was made at Boston's Logan Airport, the aircraft then flying direct to the Aeritalia base at Turin where support was provided for the tour. The F&R testing commenced by flying to a number of Italian cities, when the aircraft was also flown by Aeritalia test pilots and airline pilots with Alitalia and

Ethiopian. During the Middle East part of the tour, the aircraft was flown by HM King Hussein of Jordan and later visits were made to Luton and Oslo to familiarise the staff of, respectively, Britannia Airways and Braathens SAFE, the two European customers. On 20 July the aircraft left Oslo for a direct flight to Seattle, establishing a new non-stop distance record for twin-jet airliners. With a gross take-off weight of 317,000lb, including a 30,500lb payload, the 767 flew the 4,333nm at an average speed of 507mph. The operating altitudes varied from 35,000-41,000ft, and headwinds of up to 80mph were encountered. The elapsed flight time was 9hr 50min and on landing 12,800lb of fuel remained in the tanks.

During the flight test programme results consistently demonstrated a better performance than predicted, the most significant areas of improvement being in lower drag than originally calculated, and the empty weight less than forecast. Noteworthy improvements were found with airfield performance, altitude capability, fuel consumption and maximum range. The late decision to adapt from three to two-crew operation presented a major challenge to Boeing to modify the first 30 aircraft, while maintaining existing delivery schedules. The flight testing burden of this

change was somewhat eased by the 757 development programme, using what was to become a virtually identical two-crew cockpit. The 767 was certificated to an initial take-off weight of 300,000lb powered by a pair of JT9D-7R4 turbofans for two-crew operation. By this time 24 Boeing 767s had rolled off the final assembly line at Everett, followed by a move into the modification area for the flightdeck changes, with a schedule calling for 25 aircraft to be delivered to seven customers by the end of 1982.

The 767 completed its flight testing; its pleasant flying characteristics resembled a larger 737. It was easy to fly and manoeuvre by hand with light control forces, and free from the feeling of great bulk associated with large aircraft like the 747. The virtually identical cockpits of both the 757 and 767 offered a marked improvement in visibility and noise level over earlier Boeings. A major achievement by the design office, proven during flight testing, was to make the two aircraft fly alike, despite differences in wing size and sweep, and in the lateral control systems. This allowed a common type rating for the pilots of airlines operating both aircraft, improving crew rostering flexibility and reducing crew training costs. The US FAA approved a common type rating for the two aircraft on 22 July 1983.

With such relatively low initial sales figures on both the Boeing 757 and 767, compared with estimates, there was a need for cost effective improvements which would widen the market penetration without involving too high an investment. By increasing the all up weight of the standard 767-200 and using the wing centre-section for fuel the -200ER (Extended Range) version was produced for modest cost, giving the aircraft a trans-Atlantic capability for the less busy schedules.

Boeing planned a 6,000nm-range for the 767s for service entry in the 1990s, highlighting the over-water twin-engined controversy. Such a range would give no limitations at all for major over-water routes. This could be achieved with improved engine reliability and better systems redundancy by the addition of a hydraulically driven electrical generator fed by engine driven pumps, assuming that at least one engine is always running. If all engine driven services fail, the APU would still provide both electrical and hydraulic power, the relight envelope being extended from 35,000-40,000ft.

The most obvious external change to the Boeing 767 is the lengthening of the fuselage by 21ft 1in to accommodate another 50 passengers at the same gross weight as the -200ER of 345,000lb. This version known as the 767-300 was ordered initially by Japan Airlines on 29 September 1983, which specified four aircraft powered by the 48,000lb-thrust Pratt & Whitney JT9D-7R4D engines. In mid-October 1986 a further six 767-300s were added to the order.

The first -300 was rolled out on 14 January 1986, making its maiden flight on the 30th of the month from Paine Field adjacent to the Everett final assembly plant. Certification of this new variant was completed in eight months on 22 September after 430hr of flight testing. Delivery of the first aircraft to Japan Airlines, the third 767-300 built — JA 8234 — was on 25 September. It was also the 150th 767 to be completed.

Boeing has also proceeded with development of the extended range 767-300ER, combining a further structural strengthening with additional wing fuel tankage and being powered by the new generation 60,000lb-thrust CF6-80C2 or Pratt & Whitney PW4056 engines. The nacelles are common to the 747-400. Initially the 767-300ER had a 380,000lb gross weight, giving it an equivalent range to the 767-200ER, but improvements were made on a 400,000lb configuration with 500 miles greater range. The new engines give the -300ER a five per cent improvement in economy over the standard -300.

Although not a development, but more a modification of the standard 767-200 airframe, the US Army Airborne Optical Adjunct (AOA) is used as a technology demonstration system in the Strategic Defense Initiative (SDI) programme. A new 86ft-long upper-deck contains infra-red sensors for the detection and tracking of incoming intercontinental ballistic missile (ICBM) re-entry vehicles, while the existing main deck contains data processing and control equipment. To help balance the aerodynamic loads of the 7.7ft-high cupola, the height of the fin was also increased. Modification work on the Boeing 767 commenced in early 1987 for flight trials in 1988 and 1989, the 767 being particularly suitable for this task due to its good high altitude performance and very accurate and stable auto pilot. With the final closure of the Boeing 707 airframe production at the end of 1991, the 767 airframe was selected as the platform for future AWACs orders, Japan being an early prospect.

Below:
Following assembly of the major structural components, the Boeing 767s are equipped on an adjacent track. The rudders are painted prior to assembly.

4. The 757 Design and Development

During the six months or so which elapsed between the decision to go ahead with the 757 and the signature of final contracts with British Airways and Eastern Airlines, Boeing was able to plan the start of the manufacturing programme, which commenced on 23 March 1979. During this formative period and the few months to follow, two important configuration changes were made, as well as a number of other refinements. These two changes were the adoption of the common flightdeck with the 767 (rather than have commonality on the older types the 757 was intended to replace); and the abandonment of the T-tail layout in favour of a conventional fuselage-mounted tailplane. This was to meet the changing stability and control requirements of the longer aircraft with wing-mounted engines. The low tail layout gave an 18ft reduction in overall length, for the same cabin capacity, offering, amongst other things, a major advantage in ground manoeuvrability. This later change was only agreed a few days before contract signature by the launch airlines.

Design maximum take off weight of the 757 as initially produced was 220,000lb with customary weight growth planned in two steps, to 230,000lb with minor modifications for existing aircraft after a year, and an optional 240,000lb on new production aircraft.

Since the wing and centre sections were already full of fuel there was little scope for increasing the fuel capacity by a substantial amount, the increase in gross weights helping more in difficult airfield situations. Where there are no runway restrictions, the higher gross weight allows 178 passengers on US domestic operations to be flown 3,080nm, instead of 2,150nm. Carrying 223 passengers on international operations, the range is increased from 1,610nm to 2,520. The take-off field lengths required at sea level and a temperature of 84°F (29°C), range from 6,870ft at the basic weight to 7,610ft at 230,000lb and 8,410ft at the top weight.

With about 70% of all air travel consisting of flights of less than two hours duration, and most short-haul travellers wanting times that fit their schedules, it is important for an airline to offer a high daily frequency. It, therefore, makes sense to fly frequent trips with a comparatively small airliner rather than a few trips with a larger aircraft.

The 757 was conceived at a time of ever rising fuel prices, making efficiency the greatest factor in the design requirement. The use of the right turbofan engine can give a fuel saving in the order of 20%, but aerodynamic and other airframe improvements are worth about another 10%. By retaining the narrow body six-abreast fuselage profile of the 727, seven percent was saved over a seven-abreast twin-aisle aircraft. Passenger appeal is of course a critical factor, but it appears that for any trips under two hours a narrow body is acceptable, according to the Boeing market research. The 757 was optimised for a 500nm sortie with average sector times below two hours. Typical customers, many of whom could be existing 727 operators, would have fuel economy as a priority and would be less interested in the larger cargo capability offered by wide bodied airliners.

Although the 757 lacked any direct competition, the McDonnell Douglas DC-9 Super 80 was the closest threat, and with its lower costs, offered the financially hard pressed airlines a cost effective answer to their requirements, at least in the short term. The proposed 150-seat Airbus A320 was likely to be a threat at the lower end of the market when it entered service.

The commonality of design features between the 757 and 767 was a logical step with the two aircraft being produced almost simultaneously, even if they were the responsibility of different design teams. This not only reduced development costs, but made the aircraft more attractive to airlines planning to operate both types.

The 757 wing uses basically the same aerofoil section as the 767, except that it is smaller in overall size and is thinner where it joins the fuselage. The section is aft loaded with a comparatively flat top, and a small under surface cusp towards the trailing edge. The benefits include a delayed Mach drag-rise, less wing sweep and a more efficient wing structure. Both the new Boeings were designed for a Mach 0.8 cruise, but the significantly reduced wing sweep back is

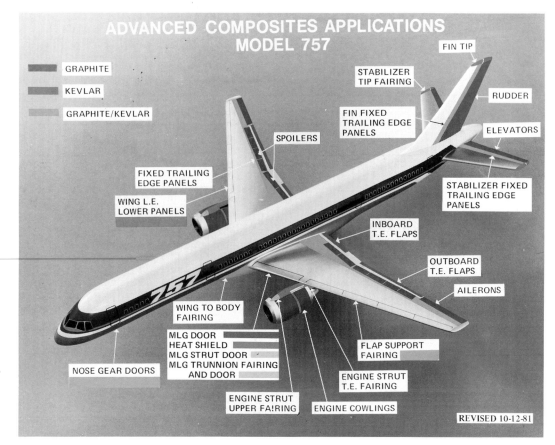

ADVANCED COMPOSITES APPLICATIONS
MODEL 757

GRAPHITE

KEVLAR

GRAPHITE/KEVLAR

FIN TIP

STABILIZER
TIP FAIRING

RUDDER

FIN FIXED
TRAILING EDGE
PANELS

SPOILERS

ELEVATORS

FIXED TRAILING
EDGE PANELS

STABILIZER FIXED
TRAILING EDGE
PANELS

WING L.E.
LOWER PANELS

INBOARD
T.E. FLAPS

OUTBOARD
T.E. FLAPS

AILERONS

WING TO BODY
FAIRING

MLG DOOR
HEAT SHIELD
MLG STRUT DOOR
MLG TRUNNION FAIRING
AND DOOR

FLAP SUPPORT
FAIRING

NOSE GEAR DOORS

ENGINE STRUT
T.E. FAIRING

ENGINE STRUT
UPPER FAIRING

ENGINE COWLINGS

REVISED 10-12-81

Above:
Advanced composites are used extensively on non-primary structure components in the Boeing 757.

25%, compared with 32.5% on the 767. The lower sweep was tolerated without a large drag penalty, because of the 757's lower average speed caused by a significant part of each flight either climbing or descending. Boeing was able to avoid the complexity of inboard ailerons, the wing being stiffer, raising the aileron reversal speed. The 757 has a generous wing area giving an easier capability of stretch to the fuselage, and at the same time eases accommodation of the undercarriage. The larger wing span reduces induced drag. The shorter sectors allow the 757 to use sophisticated high lift devices, such as double-slotted flaps and full-span slats, without cruise drag penalty. The two engines are mounted on underwing pylons to relieve bending movement and the shortened fuselage, achieved with the low set tailplane, eliminates the chance of ineffective pitch control at nose-up altitudes.

As with the 767, the airframe design goal was for 50,000 flights, the equivalent of 20 years of airline service. The Boeing structural philosophy was the built up approach which involved more tooling and assembly labour when compared with the European emphasis on integrally machined parts. About 35-40% of the 757 was created in the design stage by computer aided design, following the lead established by the 767.

Composite materials and improved aluminium alloys reduced the weight of each 757 by about 2,000lb giving an average fuel saving per year of up to 30,000 US gallons, assuming typically 1,400 trips, each of 1,000nm. The two main composites were carbon fibre-reinforced plastic (CFRP) and Kevlar-reinforced plastic. The CFRP applications included elevators, rudder, ailerons, spoilers and engine cowlings. A hybrid of CFRP and Kevlar was used for the majority of access panels, undercarriage doors and the wing/fuselage and flap track fairings. Kevlar-reinforced plastic was used for some access panels, engine pylon fairings, and fin and tailplane tip fairings.

The new aluminium alloys offered between 5-13% better strength, without any reduction in fatigue properties, toughness or corrosion resistance. The increased strength is gained by a tighter control of the amounts of copper and zinc

MAKE/BUY PLAN
MODEL 757-200

LEGEND:

JANUARY 1990

- RENTON
- WICHITA
- VERTOL
- VOUGHT
- CASA
- DUNLOP
- FLEET INDUSTRIES
- GOODRICH
- GRUMMAN
- ISRAEL AIRCRAFT INDUSTRIES
- AUBURN
- NIPPI
- ASTA
- HAWKER DE HAVILLAND
- HEATH TECNA
- HITCO
- MENASCO
- ROHR
- ROLLS ROYCE / PRATT
- SCHWEIZER
- SHORT BROTHERS
- RENTON / SOKO

NOTE:
This graphic is intended soley for quick identification. This is not a comprehensive list of program suppliers.

Above:
The production break-down of the Boeing 757 showing the wide industrial and geographical shift of production responsibility. However, the major part of the aircraft is Boeing-built at Renton.

in the alloy, the major structural areas being wing skins, stringers and lower spar booms. Boeing used 3,340lb of composites in the 757 giving a weight saving of 1,490lb. A further 610lb was saved by using 11,380lb of improved aluminium. In a stringent weight reducing programme, 1,500lb was saved during three years of design, allowing a significant increase in range, opening up routes between Europe and the Middle East.

A full size 757 test airframe was subjected to a comprehensive fatigue test programme, being simulated in a total time of 14 months, representing 100,001 flights and 40 years in airline operation.

The Boeing systems philosophy calls for the minimum crew action following a failure, with the majority of transfers made automatically to standby units. The engine indication and crew alerting system (EICAS) demonstrates this by making little provision for trouble shooting, which is justified by the high level of built-in automation, and the inability of the crew to make any adjustments once a fault has been traced.

This philosophy implies comparatively simple systems, and a two fuel tank approach would have been preferred. However, because of the smaller wing, to maintain a useful range, fuel has to be carried in the centre section, extending almost as far outboard as the engine pylons. To maintain bending movement relief, the fuel in the outer wing tanks is used last.

There are three hydraulic systems: one driven by each engine and the other by electric pumps using engine generated electricity. The pumps are the same type as those used on the 767. Two 90kVA Sundstrand-supplied generators are the heart of the electrical system, also common to the bigger aircraft. As on the 767, electric signalling, rather than control cables, operate the spoilers.

Although the Rolls-Royce RB211-535 cropped fan engine developing 37,400lb of thrust was the lead engine, largely because it had the advantage of being already certificated, alternatives were offered. Following the launch orders by British Airways and Eastern, who selected the

Rolls-Royce engine, two small orders were received from Transbrasil and Aloha specifying the General Electric CF6-32C1 rated at 36,500lb thrust. Although offering slightly less power, this was compensated by a lower weight and it was about a year behind the British engine in its certification programme. However, the Aloha order was cancelled, and with further substantial orders from American Airlines and Delta specifying the Pratt & Whitney PW2037 engines developing 38,200lb thrust, the GE engine was no longer economic to certificate unless a substantial order was received. As a result, Transbrasil adopted the PW2037 engines.

The Pratt & Whitney engine had, in fact, emerged as a prospective power plant in late 1980 and started as the newly developed JT10D rather than a scaled down JT9D. With fuel economy as a major consideration in the operation of modern airliners, the competition between the engine manufacturers was very keen, as each stood to gain a major slice of business, not only on initial sales, but spares, support and replacement engines during the aircraft life cycle. Fuel burn figures for the 757 were estimated by Boeing to be as low as 59lb per seat on a 500nm US domestic one-class seating trip, 44lb per seat on a 400nm international one-class seating trip and 93-102lb per seat on a 1,000nm flight. The comparisons with the earlier generation aircraft are even more dramatic, the 737-200 using 21-25% more fuel per passenger, and the 727-200 which used 36-39% more fuel per passenger than the 757. With fuel accounting for an ever-increasing proportion of aircraft operating costs, these figures have a high significance and the credit is shared by the manufacturers of the fuel efficient engines and the designers of a low drag airframe. British Airways stated that the 757 was, by a useful margin, the cheapest seat/mile performer of any of the aircraft considered in its detailed and protracted evaluation.

Boeing produced nearly half the parts of the first 200 aircraft, the remainder being supplied by

Flightdeck Arrangement

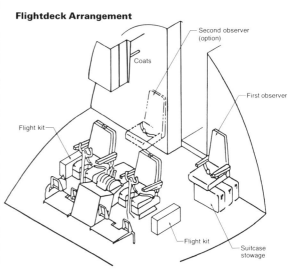

Pilots' Main Panel

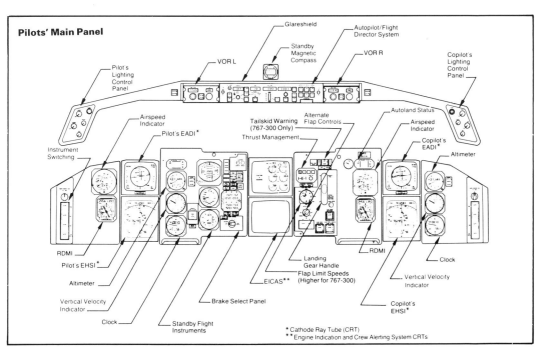

* Cathode Ray Tube (CRT)
** Engine Indication and Crew Alerting System CRTs

31

Attitude Director Indicator

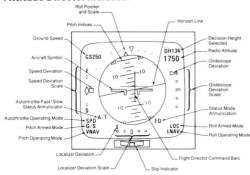

Roll Pointer and Scale
Pitch Indices
Horizon Line
Ground Speed
Decision Height Selected
Radio Altitude
Aircraft Symbol
DH134
1750
GS250
Glideslope Deviation
Speed Deviation
Speed Deviation Scale
Glideslope Deviation Scale
Autothrottle Fast/Slow Status Annunciator
A/T
Status Mode Annunciation
Autothrottle Operating Mode
SPD
G/S
VNAV
LOC
LNAV
F D
Pitch Armed Mode
Roll Armed Mode
Pitch Operating Mode
Roll Operating Mode
Localizer Deviation
Flight Director Command Bars
Localizer Deviation Scale
Slip Indicator

Horizontal Situation Indicator — Map Mode

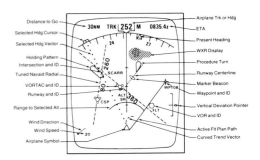

Distance to Go
30NM TRK 252 M 0835.4z
Airplane Trk or Hdg
Selected Hdg Cursor
ETA
Selected Hdg Vector
Present Heading
WXR Display
Holding Pattern Intersection and ID
SCARR
Procedure Turn
Tuned Navaid Radial
Runway Centerline
VORTAC and ID
Marker Beacon
WPT08
Runway and ID
ALT
9R
Waypoint and ID
Range to Selected Alt
CSP
FLT
Vertical Deviation Pointer
VOR and ID
Wind Direction
Active Flt Plan Path
Wind Speed
20
Curved Trend Vector
Airplane Symbol

Electronic Flight Instrument System

The Electronic Flight Instrument System (EFIS) comprises the Attitude Director Indicator (ADI) and the Horizontal Situation Indicator (HSI) and their associated symbol generator (SG) and control panel. These electronic instruments provide aircraft attitude and positioning information to the crew by means of cathode-ray tube (CRT) displays in seven colours. The displays are programmed by software in the symbol generator. These instruments have no moving parts and thus have a higher reliability than mechanical indicators.

Attitude Director Indicator

The ADI presents primary aircraft attitude indication as well as pitch and roll information to the flight crew. In addition, other ancillary data is displayed (ie, ground speed, autopilot, auto-throttle and flight director modes, etc). The ADI in conjunction with the Horizontal Situation Indicator (HSI) presents complete aircraft attitude and position information to the pilots.

Horizontal Situation Indicator

The Horizontal Situation Indicator (HSI) can be operated in any of four basic modes: Map mode, VOR mode. ILS mode and Plan mode, and an optional Compass Rose mode.

The HSI depicts the horizontal positioning of the aircraft in relation to selected flight data and a map of navigation features. The aircraft track, trend vector indication and desired flight plan path indicate the relation of aircraft position to desired position. This allows rapid and accurate (manual or automatic) flight path correction and manoeuvring by the crew. Indications of other data such as wind speed/direction, lateral and vertical deviation (from selected vertical profile), estimated time to the next waypoint, etc are also displayed as required.

Map Mode

In the Map mode, weather radar returns may be superimposed on the HSI. The scale for the map is selected on the EFIS control panel. The weather presentation is colour coded to define precipitation density: green — least dense; yellow — moderate density; and red — most intense. The weather radar presentation is automatically scaled and oriented to agree with the selected HSI display. ADF pointers are displayed when an ADF signal is being received. Provision for an optional weather radar indicator separate from the HSI is provided on the aisle stand forward of the throttles.

Below:
Flight development of the Boeing 757 was conducted from the flight test centre at Paine Field, Everett.

Horizontal Situation Indicator — ILS Mode

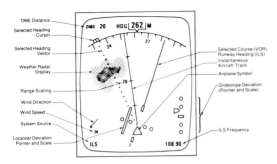

Horizontal Situation Indicator — Compass Rose Mode

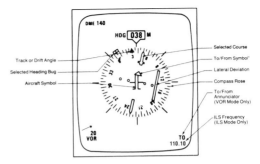

VOR and ILS Modes

The HSI in the VOR mode depicts the relationship of the aircraft with respect to a selected VOR course. The lateral deviation is in relation to a selected VOR course. When the ILS mode is selected, the presentation is similar; however, deviation is shown from ILS localiser course and glideslope. Weather radar returns may be presented on the HSI in proper scale in the same manner as for the Map mode presentation.

Plan Mode

The Plan mode enables the presentation of north-up static map display. In the Plan mode, any portion of the flight plan stored in the FMC data base can be displayed, and the display is centred on a waypoint selected by the FMC control and display unit (CDU). Data displayed in the Plan mode includes all data defined for the Map mode except: weather radar, wind data, present position data, and predicted position data.

Compass Rose Mode (optional)

The HSI may be operated in the optional, more conventional full Compass Rose mode as well as the Map or VOR or ILS modes. This mode depicts deviation from selected VOR or ILS course. DME distance, heading, tuned frequency, wind speed and direction. Glideslope deviation is also shown, as required, with scale and pointer on the right side of the instrument. ADF pointers are displayed when an ADF signal is being received.

---

mainly US-based subcontractors. Boeing is responsible for the nose section from the Military Airplane Division at Wichita, Kansas, while the Vertol Division supplies the fixed leading edge for the wings. Wing skins, access doors, rudder and elevators, as well as final assembly are at Renton, taking over from the running down 727 production line.

Following the delivery of two 757s at the end of 1982, just over 30 were scheduled to be delivered in 1983 with production rate reaching 2.5 aircraft per month by the end of that year. Each 757-200 was expected to cost $31-34 million at 1981 prices.

The full go-ahead for the 757 came in March 1979, about nine months after the start of the 767, but because the 757 is smaller and has some systems commonality with the larger aircraft, the overall development programme was planned to take 35 months from go-ahead compared with 39 months for the 767. There was an orderly transfer of design and engineering personnel from the 767 to the 757, avoiding a short term peak in labour requirements, and all major milestones were achieved on or ahead of schedule. First metal was cut on 10 December 1979,

well ahead of schedule, and major assembly commenced at Renton in January 1981.

The flight test programme was planned to take l,284hr, 65 fewer than the 767, with certification planned before the end of 1982 to allow deliveries and service entry early the following year. Certification of the RB211-535C was expected by the end of March 1981.

Flight testing of the 757 commenced a week ahead of schedule with its maiden flight from Renton on 19 February 1982. The Boeing-owned first production aircraft, N757A, was the first of five 757s to take part in the certification programme, and after its initial flight of 2hr 31min, it landed at the flight test centre at Everett's Paine Field. The project test pilot, John Armstrong, who commanded the first flight assessed the aircraft as simple to handle and all the first flight goals were achieved including the checking of all the high lift devices and taking the aircraft to a maximum IAS of 250kt. This was also the first flight of the Boeing new technology two-man cockpit.

The 757 immediately commenced an intensive flight test programme aimed at FAA certification by December of the same year. However, the

poor late winter weather of Washington State restricted the schedule to fair weather only in the initial stages to avoid undue risk with a new aircraft. Boeing's commercial flight test director, Lew Wallick, was also on the first flight, and having already flown the 767 was soon optimistic of the common type rating on both aircraft. The 757 was easy to formate on the 727 camera aircraft, and the early part of the programme included high-speed, low-speed and manoeuvring stability checks. Much of the testing concentrated on the new flightdeck avionics shared with the 767, but the 757 was leading the way in this respect. The new flat-screen cathode ray tube displays were easy to read, easy to use, were well lit even in bright light, without glare at night and did not suffer from parallax.

The first non-Boeing pilot to fly the 757 was HRH the Duke of Edinburgh in April 1982, during a visit to Seattle. He shared this flight with Lew Wallick in the right hand seat, giving some idea of the confidence in the new aircraft. By early May, the second aircraft, the first for Eastern Airlines, had joined the programme for type certification. The second to the fifth of Eastern 757s were all used during the development pro-

gramme for the certification of the RB211-535-powered version, followed later by the PW2037-powered 757s for Delta. By mid-1982, over 200hr had been flown, including noise monitoring, take-off, landing and cruise performance testing, with encouraging results. Minimum unstick velocity tests, with the tail skid scraping the runway to avoid stalling on take-off were undertaken at the vast Edward's Air Force Base in California. During these tests, chief test pilot, John Armstrong, completed 28 tail-dragging minimum speed take-offs during one week, the rear fuselage being protected by an oak skid.

By August, the first aircraft for British Airways was in final assembly, to be allocated to UK CAA certification testing. It made its first flight of 2hr 23min from Renton in late October when its test schedule included initial flight control and engine testing and a fully automatic touch and go at Moses Lake airport.

The flight test programme progressed so well that the fifth aircraft for Eastern was able to participate in a sales tour to southeast Asia, including Japan Airlines, in August. The same aircraft participated in the Farnborough Air Show in September as part of a demonstration tour of

Europe. During October and November, this 757 completed an intensive 16 nation tour of Africa, Europe, the Middle East and North and South America. A total distance of 46,660nm were covered in 67 flights with no aircraft related delays. During the Scandinavian part of the tour, automatic landings in high-crosswind conditions were demonstrated at Stockholm and Copenhagen. The longest flight of the tour was the 3,941 mile sector from Miami to Buenos Aires, overflying Cuba, Panama, Ecuador and Bolivia. By mid-November, on completion of this tour, about 1,200 flying hours had been completed in the development programme, with the fourth aircraft being refurbished before delivery to Eastern Airlines, having completed its flight testing tasks.

As the results were obtained from the flight test programme, the 757 was found to be three percent better on fuel burn than predicted, a 200nm improvement in range and an operating weight some 3,650lb below the original 1979 specification. The aircraft was proving to be the most fuel efficient of any airliner currently available over a 1,000nm sector. Meanwhile the first 757s for two British charter operators, Monarch Airlines and Air Europe, were in final assembly in December, both for delivery in March 1983.

FAA certification was achieved for the 757 on 17 December 1982, with the first aircraft for Eastern delivered. CAA approval followed in January 1983, allowing British Airways to commence service from London to Belfast on 9 February 1983.

As commercial operations built up, some US airlines began using 757s on transcontinental services, encouraging the trend to develop this aircraft for extended range operations. Eastern Airlines used the 4,550 mile range with full payload to fly between Newark, near New York, to Los Angeles and San Francisco. Northwest Airlines operate 757s between Washington Dulles and Seattle. Delta is operating between Atlanta and Seattle, as well as using the 757 for shorter trips.

The main development trends for the 757 have been as a combi or package freighter. In fact,

Left:
Production of the narrow-body 757 is at the Boeing plant at Renton, where all the earlier narrow-bodied airliners have been built.

Right:
The Boeing 757 featured a single-aisle, six-abreast seating arrangement in the passenger cabin.

Far right:
The 757 cabin provides ample carry-on baggage stowage in overhead lockers.

Below right
A major development of the 757 was the all-cargo Package Freighter for UPS. The features of this type included deleted windows, a forward upward opening cargo door on the port side and a smaller crew entry door moved forward. One of the type, N409UP, is seen at Clearwater, Florida in November 1989. *P. J. Birtles*

United Parcel ordered 20 of this latter version on 31 December 1985 powered by the PW2037 engines, with options on a further 15, the total value of the contract being $850 million. This order was sufficient to launch the 757PF which can carry up to 14 88x125in containers at 520lb and 440cu ft each plus two unique containers on the main deck. With a maximum take-off weight of 240,000lb, the 757-200PF can carry a total of 8,080lb of cargo, the main-deck volume of 6,680cu ft being supplemented by a further lower-deck bulk volume of 1,830cu ft.

Following a survey of the overnight package market in the USA and the possible interest of the US Post Office in early 1985, Boeing found enough interest to expect a market for 70-100 aircraft. By designing and developing an aircraft specifically for freight carrying, rather than converting from passenger use, Boeing produced a more cost effective aircraft. The 10,000lb higher gross weight to 250,000lb over the passenger version allows about 600nm increase in range. The 41,700lb thrust PW2040 engines have a thrust increase of about five percent to achieve economic operations out of the UPS base at Louisville. The higher gross weight also gives the aircraft a trans-Atlantic capability independent of any 60, 90 or 120min rule due to the lack of passengers. UPS does, however, plan to equip its oceanic twins with the extended range operations package similar to the modifications to the 767-200ER. These changes include modifications to the APU, cargo bay fire suppression, the addition of a hydraulic motor generator and software changes in the EICAS. The UPS aircraft are also equipped for the provision of an auxiliary fuel tank in the lower aft cargo bay to add a further 800-900gall of fuel. Carbon brakes have been selected to save 800lb of weight. A surprise move in December 1991 was the selection by UPS of the Rolls-Royce RB211-535 engine for the 20 757PFs currently on order for delivery between 1994 and 1997. Options on these engines were also taken for a further 41 757s replacing the previous selection of the PW2040.

Above:
Launch customer for the 757PF was United Parcel Service, which has currently a total of 55 aircraft on order, some powered by Pratt & Whitney engines and others by Rolls-Royce.

Right:
Zambian Airways leased a 757PF from Ansett Worldwide Aviation in 1991.

The major differences between the 757PF and the standard version are the deletion of passenger doors, windows and all interior amenities, the installation of a 134x86in cargo door forward of the port wing, a new crew access hatch (22x55in) fitted forward of the former No 1 passenger entry door, and the addition of a solid barrier separating the cockpit from the cargo area with a sliding door access to the upper-deck. The first two 757PF aircraft were delivered to UPS on 16 September 1987, and in March 1989 the operator took up 10 of its 15 options. In November 1990, UPS ordered another 25 757PFs worth $1.7 billion with deliveries through to 2001. The first non-US operator of the 757PF was Ethiopian Airlines, who took delivery of one aircraft in September 1990. They were followed by Zambian Airways who leased a 757PF from Ansett Worldwide Aviation in early 1991 for operations throughout Africa, Europe and the Middle East. A further 757PF was leased by Ansett to London Gatwick-based Anglo Cargo in September 1991, but at the time of writing this operator is experiencing financial problems and has ceased operations.

The Royal Nepal Airlines order for two 757s on 17 February 1986 specified one Combi, thus launching the Combi 757 programme. The 757-200 Combi has a mixed main-deck cargo and passenger capability, and Boeing is confident that a market exists for further Combis. Unlike the 757PF the Combi will retain all the passenger windows and doors but will have, in addition, the 134x86in cargo door on the front cabin left-hand side. Royal Nepal has also chosen the high gross weight version of the 757 at 250,000lb, powered by the Rolls-Royce engines. The 757 Combi is capable of carrying two to four 108in standard containers on the main-deck. In the three container configuration, the Combi can carry nine tons of cargo and between 123 and 148 passengers. The Royal Nepal 757 Combi made its first flight in August 1988 for delivery the following month.

5. Boeing 767 Sales and Service Entry

Following a close-run contest with the Airbus A310, United Airlines placed the launch order on 14 July 1978 with Boeing for 30 767s, plus 37 options placed in November, for service entry in mid-1982, six months ahead of the European competition. An equally hard-fought contest between Pratt & Whitney and General Electric, resulted in the selection of the P&W JT9D-7R engines, developing 44,300lb thrust. These were derated and modified versions of the power plants of the airline's 747s. The total value of the 767-200s ordered for delivery between mid-1982 and 1984 was some $1,200 million, including spares, simulators and training, of which P&W would share $200 million.

The United 767s carry a total of 197 passengers, 24 in first-class (six-abreast seats), and 173 in economy (seven-abreast). The range of 2,200 miles is sufficient for United's one-stop transcontinental operations, the critical routes being from Denver to the East Coast and Cleveland to the West Coast. The 2,900sq ft-plus wing

area gives good field performance and a 38,000ft initial cruise altitude. Take-off field length at the maximum weight of 279,500lb is 7,300ft and the landing run 4,200ft at 226,000lb. In September 1980, United converted options on nine 767s into firm orders, bringing total firm orders to 39, retaining options on 30.

On 15 November, both American Airlines and Delta announced orders and options for a total of 92 Boeing 767-200s, all 310,000lb-transcontinental aircraft powered by 48,000lb-thrust General Electric CF6-80A engines derived from the CF6-45/50 series. The American order for 30 767s with options on 20 more signalled the demise of the 777 trijet and instead of ordering 757s at the same time, more 727s were purchased. The American order was for delivery over a 28-month period starting in October 1982,

Above:
In November 1978 American Airlines placed an order for 30 767s with options on 20 more, confirming the demise of the then 777 project.

Below:
Delta selected the GE CF6-80A engines to power their 20 767s, with options on a further 32.

with the options covering delivery positions in 1983 to 1986. The unit price was $25 million at 1978 values. Delta's order was for 20 767s worth $1.7 billion with options on a further 22 for delivery between October 1982 and 1986.

The Delta and American 767s were the first with the range for non-stop trans-USA operations and with the engine orders worth $200 mil-

lion to GE, the P&W lead engine status was virtually wiped out. The total value of the orders to Boeing including the 727s was $3,100 million, the largest single day's total in the company's history.

Overall, 1978 ended as an excellent year for the Boeing order book, with four 767s and options on two more for Pacific Western Airlines (Canada's largest regional carrier) bringing total 767 sales to 84 aircraft. The first 767 was delivered in February 1983 followed by the second in June, but the airline disposed of these aircraft when a decision was made to concentrate on an all-737 fleet.

An order was received in early 1979 from International Lease Finance Corporation (Interlease for short) with a letter of intent with Boeing for 10 767s for delivery slots between mid-1983 and late 1984. The intention was to lease the aircraft outside the USA — primarily in Europe and Asia — with Interlease preparing route studies and fleet plans from its modest office in Beverly Hills with its staff of five. As the business developed, the company confirmed the options as four 767-200ERs and three of the stretched 767-300s.

In July 1979, Air Canada decided on the 767-200 powered by Pratt & Whitney engines for its domestic and regional routes. Twelve aircraft were purchased initially, with options on a further 18, following an intense eight month sales battle between Boeing and Airbus. The Air Canada 767s were the first to be ordered at the increased gross weight of 310,000lb, an addition

of 10,000lb giving a range improvement to 3,110nm with a full passenger load. Deliveries were scheduled to start in October 1982 and be completed by November 1984, the average unit price being $Can 46 million.

The first order from outside North America came from All Nippon Airways of Japan in October 1979 for 25 767-200s and options on a further 15. The value of the contract was $1,500 million, not including the engines. The order for the engines followed in February 1980, ANA going for the GE CF6-80 (worth $150 million), putting these engine orders well ahead of Pratt & Whitney. The 767s are configured in a 229 passenger one-class layout to replace 727s and 737s on domestic and international routes; an example of the latter being Tokyo-Hong Kong-Manila. All Nippon was also very interested in a stretched version of the 767 and was likely to be lead customer for the type, the need being for seating for 40-45 more passengers over the Series 200. They placed their order on 26 December 1985 for 15 GE-powered -300s with options on 10 more, confirming this interest.

CP Air of Canada ordered four GE-powered 767s with options on four more, but these were replaced by 737s for the shorter haul routes giving a greater frequency.

In December 1979, after a most bitter struggle between Airbus and Boeing, Trans World Airlines selected the 767 as its medium-haul twin-jet for the 1980s. TWA ordered 10 aircraft powered by the Pratt & Whitney JT9D-7R4 engines developing 48,000lb thrust, with options on a further 10 767s. The eventual fleet size was expected to grow to around 45 aircraft. The value of the engines alone to P&W, covering the initial order and options, was more than $100 million.

During one week in March 1980, three more airlines were added to the customer list for the Boeing 767, bringing orders to 148 and options to 134 for a total of 11 airlines. Ansett Airlines of Australia ordered five 767s worth $235 million with deliveries starting in November 1982, breaking the long standing common fleet practice of the two major Australian domestic carriers (Trans-Australia Airlines having ordered four Airbus A300s). The US trunk carrier, Western Airlines, ordered six 767s with options on another six for delivery between the spring of 1983 and spring 1984, but this order was later cancelled. A significant breakthrough into the Asian market, dominated by Airbus, was an order for two 767s with the Taiwan flag carrier, China Airlines, for delivery in December 1982 and July 1983. Both Western and China Airlines specified the 48,000lb-thrust Pratt & Whitney JT9D-7R4D engines.

The first European customer for the 767 was Britannia Airways, which ordered two 767-200s in late March 1980 for delivery in 1984. Britannia chose the 310,000lb gross weight version with a

Above:
All Nippon Airways was the first customer outside North America, becoming a major operator of the 767.

Right:
TWA joined the major US trunk carriers by ordering the 767 at the end of 1979, later putting the aircraft on the trans-Atlantic extended range routes. *P. J. Birtles*

Below right:
The Ansett Group not only ordered 767s for operation by Ansett Airlines, but also for lease to other operators worldwide.

range of more than 3,100 miles allowing flights with up to 270 passengers to West African destinations. The 767s were to replace some of the older 737s. For the 1992 season, the 767 fleet size is expected to reach 15 aircraft, a seventh aircraft being ordered in October 1987, followed by the eighth in April 1988 for delivery a year later. The latter three aircraft were EROPS-equipped CF6-80A-powered. In November 1988, Britannia placed orders for eight 767s with options on a further eight, all equipped for extended range operations. Either Series 200 or 300 could be selected with the first delivery in 1990. Britannia also started new charter operations in November 1988 to Perth and Cairns in Australia.

The second European operator was Braathens which ordered two 767-200s in April 1980, with options on two more for delivery in February 1984. Pratt & Whitney supplied the engines, but in mid-1985 the airline decided to sell its two

767s because they were too big and costly for its European charter routes. Following a short lull in orders, Boeing added Avianca and Alaska International to its order book in December 1980. Alaska International, which was a specialist all-cargo Hercules operator, with considerable involvement in oil support operations in North Alaska, planned to enter the passenger carrying business by ordering two 767s with options on two more. However, this order was later cancelled.

In early 1981, it was rumoured that El Al had ordered four 767s, but this was not confirmed by Boeing until March, when an order worth $230 million was announced including two 737-200s. The 767s replaced 707s in 1983 and 1984 giving a 35% lower fuel consumption over the older aircraft. The order covered two 767-200s and two of the later 767-200ERs (Extended Range) aircraft with additional fuel in the wing centre section, powered by the Pratt & Whitney engines.

Also in March, Transbrasil's chairman announced an order for three 767s, confirmed by Boeing in August, to be used on Brazil's domestic routes. The order, worth $175 million, included five options and all were to be powered by the General Electric engines. The airline became the first non-US operator to order both the 757 and 767 with both types in operation by 1988 replacing the airline's 727s. Initial 767 delivery was planned for May 1983. Transbrasil later confirmed its five options, selecting the 767-300ER.

Ethiopian Airlines became the first African carrier to choose the 767-200ER when an order was placed in December 1981 for two aircraft for delivery in May and June 1984. Including options for two more, the value of the order was $100 million. The aircraft replaced 707s and 720s on such routes as Addis Ababa to Rome, carrying a full load of passengers and up to six tons of

cargo. One of the options became a firm order in January 1987.

There then followed a lull in 767 sales, which was not helped by an announcement, in June 1982, of United cancelling or substantially delaying 20 out of the 39 firm orders. This financially prudent step was caused by the failure of the US economy to make any significant recovery from the recession which gripped it, delays in the rebuilding of US air traffic control capacity after the government dismissals of air traffic controllers a year previously, and continued US government interference in the free market system by restricting landing slot allocations at 22 major domestic airports. Additional slots became available with the collapse of Braniff, but these were distributed by FAA lottery, leaving any benefits to luck rather than by allocation due to need and capability.

United did, however, take delivery of its first 767 on 19 August 1982, when Boeing president Malcolm T. Stamper handed over the keys to Richard J. Ferris, chairman and chief executive of United Airlines, during a ceremony at the Everett plant. The aircraft, the ninth completed on the 767 production line, was flown to San Francisco prior to inaugurating commercial services on 8 September with a flight from Chicago to Denver. With further deliveries, services of the 767s then increased to replace the less economical DC-10s on the routes to San Francisco, La-Guardia in New York and Boston.

Four more 767s were delivered to United by the end of October, and this increased to eight aircraft by early 1983. A further 11 joined the air-

line by May, the remaining 20 of the initial firm order remaining on hold for the time being. As the fleet grew, the services expanded, from October 1982, to cover Portland, Seattle, Detroit and Newark. Daily utilisation averaged 7.5hr initially, improving to 8.2hr by mid-October per aircraft. By 1 November, United served 11 US destinations. Scheduled despatch reliability for the total 767 fleet with all airlines was 95.1%. The 20 aircraft on hold were rescheduled for delivery at the rate of five per year from 1985 to 1988, instead of all deliveries being completed by the end of 1984.

The 767 sales famine was apparently broken in October 1982, when Boeing received an order, subject to Thai Government approval, for two

Below:
The first European order for 767s came from the well-established Boeing operator, Britannia Airways, to allow the airline to expand into the long-haul high-density tourist charter market. *P. J. Birtles*

Above right:
Avianca of Columbia ordered two 767-200ERs at the end of 1988 for routes to Mexico and the USA.

Right:
Transbrasil ordered 767s for domestic operations, one of their aircraft being exhibited at the Paris Air Show. *P. J. Birtles*

Below right:
The continent of Africa became another 767 region when Ethiopian Airlines ordered two aircraft for their routes to Europe.

767-200ERs from Thai Airways with a range of 3,100nm. However, as Thai Airways was already an operator of 10 Airbus A300 and at that time had two A300-600s on order, the requirement for the 767s was not confirmed.

The GE-powered 767 in Delta Airlines colours appeared at the Farnborough Air Show in September 1982, and US FAA certification was received for the CF6-80A powered 767 in early October, the Pratt & Whitney-powered aircraft having been certificated on 30 July. The certification of the GE-powered aircraft cleared the way for delivery to the launch customers, Delta and American Airlines, towards the end of October and early November. By this time, two of the Delta aircraft had flown; the first commenced its test programme in February having logged 315hr on engine certification. Their second aircraft had flown about 40hr, much of it *en route* to and from the Farnborough Air Show. The long distance flights confirmed that the fuel efficiency of the 211-passenger GE-powered aircraft was 6.6% better than expected, over a 1,000nm stage.

Above:
United took delivery of their first 767 in August 1982 and commenced domestic US operations by replacing some DC-10s on less economic routes. *P. J. Birtles*

American Airlines received its first 767 on 4 November 1982, putting it into service on 21 November on the US transcontinental route from San Francisco to New York. This 767 could carry 24 first-class passengers and 180 economy. By 1984 10 767-200s had been delivered with plans for three in 1985 and 1986, four in 1987 and five each in 1988 and 1989. By the end of 1985, 13 767-200s and two 767-200ERs were in operation with American, with 10 767-200s on order for delivery between 1986 and 1988 and five -200ERs available for service during 1986,

Below:
American Airlines launched the 767-300ER for their North Atlantic routes commencing with Manchester in 1988, prior to slots at Heathrow becoming available. The 767-200ERs had paved the way the previous year, an example being N332AA seen at Manchester in October 1987. *P. J. Birtles*

Above:
With the improved economic situation, Air Canada ordered 767-200ERs for the North Atlantic routes, thereby replacing TriStars. C-GDSP is seen on approach to Heathrow in April 1992. *P. J. Birtles*

covering the original order for 30 aircraft. American Airlines launched the larger 767-300ER powered by the CF6-80C2 engines with 215 seats for the new European services. Deliveries commenced in early 1988, and 11 more -300ERs were ordered in mid-1991.

The third airline to take delivery of the 767, and the first outside the USA, was Air Canada on 30 October 1982. The aircraft were acquired to replace the airline's DC-8s which were phased out by mid-1983. However, it was not a smooth introduction, as the airline's pilots refused to fly the new aircraft on the route proving programme in preparation for the start of regular scheduled services on 1 January 1983. This date was delayed while negotiations continued over new rates of pay, as the airline had offered the pilots lower salaries for flying the 767 than the DC-8. The reason given by the airline was the perceived lower work load, despite the lack of a flight engineer. By the end of January 1983 a tentative agreement had been reached and this was ratified by the Canadian Airline Pilots Association. This allowed the first two aircraft, which had been grounded at Toronto and Montreal, to start full commercial services on 14 February. The first aircraft operated Toronto-Calgary and Calgary-Toronto-Montreal-San Francisco and San Francisco-Toronto routes. However, by July 1983, Air Canada postponed indefinitely its options on six 767s due to poor prevailing market conditions, Canada's general economic recession and financial reasons. Substantial cutbacks had been made with some routes, and frequencies had been reduced on others. By this time, Air Canada had four 767s in operation with two more joining the fleet by the end of the year. When the market improved, Air Canada ordered four 767-200ERs in July 1987 with options on six more, for delivery to commence the next year. A year later, three more -200ERs worth about $170 million were ordered in addition to the 15 already held on option, and in September 1989 six more -300ERs were ordered with nine options.

Delta had been profitable for 37 out of the past 38 years up to the end of 1985. It is one of the largest airlines in the USA carrying 37 million passengers a year to 106 cities in the USA, Canada, Bermuda, the Bahamas, Britain, West Germany and France. The 39,000 employees are largely non-union with a strong loyalty to the airline. When Delta made its first quarterly financial loss in mid-1982, due to declining traffic and other problems, it did not lay off any employees, like its competition. To show their gratitude, the Delta staff, on their own initiative, raised $30 million to pay for the first Boeing 767. This was achieved by authorising a percentage of payroll deductions over one year and by direct contributions. The aircraft, N102DA, together with N103DA, was delivered on 25 October 1982 and named *The Spirit of Delta*. Delta's principal hub is at Atlanta where 767 services commenced on 15 December. The 767 fleet plans in early 1986 had been adjusted slightly to 15 Series 200s, the last of which N115DA was delivered on 28 February 1984, to be followed by nine Series 300 ordered on 21 February 1984, plus 18 on option. The Series 200 had seats for 18 first-class passengers and 186 tourist, totalling 204. The Series 300 could carry 25 first-class and 320 tourist-class passengers. Delta ordered six more 767-300s in May 1987 with deliveries starting the following February. In September 1988 Delta placed a series of major orders for new aircraft including nine 767-300ERs with options on 16 more. In mid-1991 Delta confirmed two more -300ERs, taking its total to 59 Boeing 767s.

Delta added the 767-300 to their fleet when they placed orders for the stretched high-capacity version in February 1984.

TWA had its first 767 delivered on 22 November 1982 and daily scheduled services were commenced between Dulles Airport at Washington DC, San Francisco and Los Angeles on 9 December. By early June 1986 six 767s had been supplied to TWA.

Pacific Western Airlines took delivery of the first of four of its 767s on 4 March 1983 with the second aircraft in early June. The 767 order book was further reduced in April 1984 when Pacific Western substituted four 737s for one of two 767s it still had on order. By this time, China Airlines had received its first 767 on 20 December 1982 and All Nippon two aircraft, the first on 25 April.

In the spring of 1983, the battle between Airbus and Boeing was continuing in the international airline market with Gulf Air and MEA as prospects. Other airlines in the Middle East region such as Alia Jordanian and a number of African operators could follow.

China Airlines commenced its 767 services on 1 January 1983, on the Taipei-Hong Kong-Bangkok route, with special permission to overfly Vietnam, achieving load factors in excess of 90%. Although Ansett had expected its first delivery in November 1982, with services commencing the next month, the continuing recession resulted in deliveries being delayed. The first aircraft arrived on 7 June 1983 with three more by August. Meanwhile, the 315,000lb maximum take-off weight 767 was certificated by the FAA in June, the 15,000lb increase allowing a 2,000lb greater payload or 760 statute miles greater range. China Airlines was the first operator to receive this improvement, and all the 52 767s delivered to date could be operated at the new weight providing FAA approved changes were made to the flight manuals.

The first commercial 767 operation in Europe was started by El Al with their initial 767 on its delivery flight from Seattle on 12 July 1983. It arrived at Heathrow and collected 100 passengers bound for Tel Aviv; the first of four aircraft inaugurating the twice weekly service, which commenced in November, between the two destinations. In the meantime, it replaced the airline's 707s on the African and some European routes, with accommodation for 224 passengers, 18 business-class and 206 tourist-class. The second 767 was delivered in September and the third and fourth aircraft, delivered in 1984, were the extended range version for use on the trans-Atlantic routes.

In its first year of operation, the 767 escaped from two near disasters. The first of these happened in late July 1983, when Air Canada 767 C-GUAN with 61 passengers and eight crew on board ran out of fuel en route from Ottawa to Edmonton. An emergency landing was made at the former Gimli Air Force Base, about 50 miles north of Winnipeg, which had been converted to a motor racing circuit. On landing, the aircraft ran through a number of metal barriers collapsing the nose wheel, but no-one was seriously hurt.

The crew was alerted by a low fuel pressure warning while cruising at 41,000ft, and the captain started a diversion to Winnipeg. At 31,000ft one engine failed due to lack of fuel, followed by the other engine flaming out 3,000ft lower. The APU was started to maintain electrical power, but it too soon failed for lack of fuel. With the reduction in hydraulic pressure, the ram air turbine dropped down automatically, and the aircraft batteries kept all essential services and instruments operating for the 60 mile glide for about 15min.

The fuel shortage began on the ground with an unserviceability in the fuel quantity sensors, which was overcome by physical dipstick test. However, the error was made due to the reading of pounds of fuel as kilogrammes, failing to make the conversion to metric and leading the pilots to believe they had more than twice the quantity of

Top:
Qantas ordered 767s in September 1983 for domestic charter operations and extended range international scheduled routes in the Pacific market.

Right:
Qantas provided a high level of passenger comfort and service in both first and tourist-class cabins. *Qantas*

Left:
The first scheduled 767 services in Europe were started by El Al in July 1983; One of the airline's aircraft, 4X-EAB, is seen at Heathrow in October 1988.
P. J. Birtles

fuel than was actually present. Following this incident, no 767s would be allowed to operate with unserviceable fuel tank indication systems.

The second serious incident was also power related. On this occasion, a United Airlines 767 was *en route* from Los Angeles to Denver on 19 August 1983, when the captain shut down both Pratt & Whitney engines at 28,000ft, 'because they were overheating'. Both engines were subsequently relit at around 12,000ft and the aircraft safely landed at Denver with no injuries to the 197 passengers and eight crew. One engine was changed at Denver for inspection, to allow the aircraft to be ferried back to San Francisco for a full inspection of the other engine. Subsequent investigations suggested that engine icing may have been a contributory factor, although more data needed to be processed. During a descent from 41,000ft, the aircraft entered cloud at 30,000ft and the throttles were advanced to above idle to protect against icing. However, the main generators cut out leaving standby power and instruments only. The APU was started and the ram air turbine dropped out. With the rise in exhaust gas temperature, the engines were shut down at 19,900ft and 17,400ft, the relights being successful at 15,600ft and 14,500ft. This was standard procedure, but it would not normally be anticipated that all power be lost.

The sales of the 767 began to take-off again with an order from Qantas for six 767-200ERs in September 1983, together with three 747-300s. The first two 767s were planned for delivery in October 1985, the remaining four being supplied by March 1986. Qantas stated that the 767 provided the most economic means of air transport for tourists around Australia and served airports such as Adelaide, Cairns, Darwin and Townsville. This brought the 767 order book to 180 aircraft. Qantas chose the JT9D-7R4E engines developing 50,000lb thrust and providing seats for 18 business-class and up to 196 economy-class passengers. The first aircraft, VH-EAJ named *City of Wollongong*, was delivered on 3 July 1985, some three months early and the order was completed by VH-EAO, *City of Cairns*, on 31 March 1986. Commercial operations commenced on 30 July from Melbourne to Wellington in preparation for the linking of Sydney, Melbourne and Brisbane with Wellington. As the fleet grew so Christchurch and Auckland were added, followed by links to Singapore from Adelaide, Darwin and Townsville.

The 767s allowed route expansion to Noumea, followed by Manila as an extension of the New Guinea service. New routes started from 1 April 1986 included Perth-Tokyo and Brisbane-Cairns-Tokyo, the passenger loads being supplemented by perishable cargoes such as fresh meat, fruit, vegetables, and seafood on all the international routes. In May 1987 Qantas added a 767-300ER to their order with options on six more. These new aircraft were to be powered by the CF6-80C2 engines rated at 60,800lb thrust. The engines were qualified for extended range overwater operations, which was the airline's main reason for not choosing the JT9D engines used to power the earlier 767-200s. Qantas confirmed

53

options on two more 767-300ERs in November 1987, for delivery in March 1989, and firmed up another -300 ER in April 1988, followed by another in July for delivery at the end of 1989. Four more -300ERs were ordered in early 1990.

At the same time as CP Air was substituting its 767s for 737-300s, Japan Airlines chose the 767 as a DC-8 replacement on 29 September 1983. A total of nine aircraft were ordered with options on six more, as a mix of four 767-200, two -200ER and three of the new stretched -300, all worth $560 million. The order for the -300 made JAL the launch customer for this variant. The delivery schedule called for three -200s in 1986, one in 1987 and two in 1988. The -300s were delivered in 1987, and it was planned that two would be added each year from 1988 to 1991, making a total of 15 aircraft.

In November 1983 there were strong rumours, unconfirmed by Boeing, that Kuwait Airways were ordering three 767-200ERs. This was an interesting prospect, as the airline was already an Airbus 310 and A300-600 customer, the mix apparently being unnecessary for operational purposes, as the requirement could be satisfied by either one or the other manufacturers' products. In the event Kuwait Airways confirmed its order for three 767-200ERs in September 1984, and supplied Boeing with three yet to be delivered Airbus A310s in part exchange. Although the two aircraft have the same passenger capacity, the 767 had a greater range, larger cargo

Below:
Lan Chile acquired two 767-200s in mid-1986 financed by the ILFC.

Bottom:
Varig ordered six 767-200ERs with options on four more in March 1986.

capacity and was more fuel efficient. The first of the Pratt & Whitney-powered 767s was delivered on 20 March 1986, to be operated alongside the existing fleet of A310s and A300-600s. On what was claimed to be the longest flight by a commercial twinjet, the aircraft flew 7,893 statute miles, from Seattle to Kuwait on 20 July 1986, in 14hr 12min. With the rapid start of the Gulf War, Kuwait Airways could save only one 767; the

invading forces from Iraq taking the other 767-200ERs to Baghdad.

In January 1984 Egyptair confirmed its order for three 767-200ERs powered by the P&W JT9D-7R4E engines for delivery to commence in July. The Egyptair aircraft have a 5,700-mile range with full payload, the fuel capacity being increased from 16,700 US gallons to 20,000 US gallons by utilising part of the centre tank capacity. The first Egyptair 767 was delivered in 1984, replacing the carrier's 707s on Middle Eastern and European routes as well as on services to Africa. Seating is for 206 passengers in a three-class layout. This gain of three aircraft sales was more than balanced out with the cancellation by Western Airlines of the six 767s in favour of 12 new 737s. In June 1988, Egyptair announced that it was to order two 767-300ERs, and in October, a further two -200ERs were added to the order book.

Below:
The Charlotte, North Carolina-based Piedmont became an international operator with the introduction of the 767-200ERs to Gatwick in 1987. N603P is seen pushing back from the satellite in December 1987.
P. J. Birtles

Bottom:
US Air took over Piedmont and its London Gatwick operations in 1988. *Bruce Malcolm*

On a damp Wednesday, 8 February 1984, Boeing 767 G-BKVZ landed at Luton Airport as the first of what by then had become three of the aircraft type on order for Britannia Airways. The UK CAA had granted a type certificate to the 767-200 and the issue of a Certificate of Airworthiness to Britannia's first 767 followed soon after the delivery. The 273-seat cabin incorporated many innovations including central toilets, large overhead lockers, custom built galleys and video systems to provide safety information to passengers. The first commercial 767 flight by Britannia departed Luton on 18 February for Monastir in Tunisia and a week later the first 767 sortie was made from Manchester, bound for Faro. By the end of the month the second 767 had arrived and the third aircraft followed in the spring of 1985. A fourth aircraft was ordered in May 1984. The 767s were acquired for Britannia's high density routes from Luton, Gatwick and Manchester to Palma, Alicante, Malaga, Tenerife, Athens, and Corfu. The aircraft initially had a range of 2,800nm with a capability later to fly to such areas as West Africa, the Gulf, the USA and India.

El Al was the first operator of the 767-200ER when the first of its two entered service in April 1984 on the airline's European routes, later to fly direct scheduled services between Tel Aviv and Montreal.

Ethiopian Airlines took delivery of its first high gross weight (345,000lb) 767-200ER at Addis Ababa on 1 June 1984 — the 7,500-mile delivery flight from Washington DC being the longest non-stop flight to date made by a twin-engined airliner. The flight which carried 58 passengers stayed within ICAO's 90min overwater guideline throughout the 13hr 17min flight.

In July 1984, the New Zealand Government approved the purchase of three 767-200ERs for the state airline, Air New Zealand. The 220-seat mixed-class aircraft powered by the GE 50,000lb-thrust CF6-80A2 engines were scheduled for delivery in September 1985, March and September 1986 for use on the airline's services from Wellington to Singapore and Tokyo, and Christchurch-Honolulu. The first aircraft, ZK-NBA, was handed over on 3 September 1985 and services commenced 12 days later. A further -200ER was ordered in January 1987.

CAAC, the airline of the People's Republic of China, placed an order for two Boeing 767-200ERs on 23 May 1985 powered by the Pratt & Whitney JT9D-7R4E4 engines and later

increased their order by four more aircraft. The first aircraft, B-2551, was delivered on 8 October 1985 with services commencing soon after. A further four PW4052-powered 767s were ordered by CAAC in mid-1990.

The International Lease Finance Corporation ordered two 767-200ERs powered by the GE CF6-80A2 engines on 19 February 1986 for lease to LAN-Chile in a deal worth $144 million. The 767s replace two DC-10-30s in mid-1986 on the Santiago-Miami-New York and European routes.

The penetration of the South American market continued with an order from Varig Airlines of Brazil on 18 March 1986 for six 767-200ERs with options on four more. Powered by the GE 80C2 engines, deliveries were scheduled to commence in May 1987, with the remainder by the end of the year. Total value of the order was

around $400 million and with a new derivative of the CF6 engine the aircraft was capable of flying up to 6,150 statute miles with the full payload of 200 passengers. A further South American customer is TACA of El Salvador, which ordered one 767. It started services with a leased aircraft on 1 October 1985, until its own was delivered on 22 May 1986.

In July 1986 Piedmont Airlines ordered six 767-200ERs with options on six more to be powered by CF6-80C2 engines. These aircraft, with deliveries commencing in May 1987, were the carrier's first wide bodied aircraft for use on trans-Atlantic and other long-range services, starting with Charlotte, NC to London in the 1987 peak season. Piedmont were acquired by US Air in March 1987, but the full merger was delayed until March 1988 due to legal objections. Three more -200s were ordered in April, 1989, but some deliveries were delayed in 1990.

In April 1987, Lauda Air ordered the first 56,000lb-thrust PW4000-powered 767-300ER for non-stop flights from Vienna to Bangkok. The flights could then go on to Sydney or Beijing. In October 1987, Lauda Air finally won its route licence battle with the Austrian authorities, allowing an independent operator to compete with Austrian Airlines on scheduled international services. The first 767 was due to arrive in time for flights to commence on 29 April 1988, and a second aircraft was ordered for a 1989 delivery. The first aircraft was actually delivered on 2 May 1988, and soon commenced flying twice weekly to Bangkok and once a week each to Hong Kong and Sydney. A 767-300 was ordered in September 1990.

In March 1987 Rolls-Royce and Boeing agreed to consider the 60,600lb-thrust RB524-D4D engines for the 767. As a result British Airways placed an order worth $500 million in August 1987 for 11 767-300s with options on 15 more. Deliveries were to commence at the end of 1989 and would be capable of extended range operations as service experience was built up with the engines. Similar engines also powered the airline's 747-400s.

Left:
LTU Sud ordered three 767-300s in early 1989 to add to their fleet of 757s and to commence replacement of the older TriStars.

Below left:
Air Mauritius ordered two 767-200ERs for their European routes. The first aircraft was delivered in April 1988.

Below:
Air Zimbabwe operate a pair of 767-200ERs to European destinations. One of the two, Z-WPF, is caught by the photographer just touching down at Gatwick. *Bruce Malcolm*

Bottom:
LOT of Poland became the first East European operator of the Boeing 767 with two -200ERs and this -300ER, SP-LPA.

Right:
Avianca of Colombia ordered two 767-200ERs at the end of 1988 for their routes to Mexico and the USA.

Below:
Aeromaritime, the charter subsidiary of UTA, ordered two 767-200ERs, including F-GHGD seen here on its Boeing test flight, and one -300ER. Deliveries started in September 1990.

Bottom:
Air Seychelles, operating from the tiny Indian Ocean group of islands, put 767-200ER S7-AAS into service in August 1989. London Gatwick is the UK destination of their routes.
P. J. Birtles

Canadian International ordered six GE-powered 767-300ERs in April 1987. This was increased progressively to eight -300ERs with 16 options, with a further order in January 1988 for two -200ERs and options on eight more. Two of the 16 options for -300ERs were converted to firm orders in October 1988.

It was reported that Gulf Air were to lease a pair of 767-300s in June and November 1988 for their long-haul routes. This was confirmed in March 1988; the aircraft were to be used in the USA, Australia and Japan. The first of the Gulf Air 767s was delivered on 20 June 1988 from Seattle to Bahrain, a distance of 8,085 miles in 14hr 32min. In August, Gulf Air decided to purchase four 767s to replace their TriStars, and in April 1989 ordered six 767-300ERs with options on 12 more.

Orders began picking up significantly in 1988 with SAS ordering nine 767s with 15 options in January. The order was worth $1.8 billion with deliveries starting in March 1989 for the trans-Atlantic routes. The firm orders were for seven -300ERs carrying 209 passengers in two classes up to 6,900 miles, and two -200ERs carrying 150 passengers in two classes up to 7,200 miles. These aircraft were to be powered by the PW4000 engines. The 767s were selected by SAS over the MD-11 and A340 to achieve earlier deliveries. The first three -300ERs were to be allocated to the New York and Chicago routes, later ones replacing earlier aircraft types on the routes to Seattle, Los Angeles, Bangkok, Singapore and Beijing. The -200ERs were for the thinner routes to Rio de Janeiro and Tokyo. SAS ordered four 767-300ERs in early 1989 with three more at the end of the year. In the same month LTU of Germany ordered three 767-300s worth $205 million, powered by PW4000 engines for delivery starting a year later. Martinair followed with an order for two PW4000-powered -300ERs.

On 18 April 1988, Boeing set a new world distance record in the 767 weight class, by flying the first Air Mauritius high gross weight 767-200ER the 8,727 miles (14,044km) non-stop from Halifax, Nova Scotia to Mauritius. The average speed was 460kt (853km/h) and the take-off weight was 158,400kg including 73 tonnes of fuel. It landed with seven tonnes remaining, enough for a further two hours of flying. The Air Mauritius 767s were configured for 203 passengers in a three-class layout for the 13hr non-stop flights to London. With the arrival of the second aircraft, the 767s entered service in May, bringing new destinations in Europe and Asia within non-stop reach of the Indian Ocean island, as well as serving mainland Africa.

In July 1988 Olympic Airways ordered three 767-200ERs powered by Pratt & Whitney engines, following competition with the Airbus A310-300, to replace the Boeing 707s. However, in March 1990 this order was changed to Boeing 737-400s due to reduced passenger demand.

Air Zimbabwe ordered one 767-200ER in August 1988, powered by 56,750lb-thrust PW4056 engines. In April 1989 they exercised their two options for delivery in August 1990.

The 767-300ER was now achieving the majority of sales for the type with total orders by October 1988 for 307 767s with 236 delivered. The production rate was running at three aircraft per month, and included in the overall total sales were 107 -300s of which 56 were the extended range variant.

In addition to the 11 already on order, British Airways ordered six more -300s with six options in October 1988. With the opening up of Eastern Europe, LOT of Poland became the first of the ex-Iron Curtain countries to select western airline equipment. In November 1988 they ordered two -200ERs and one -300ER powered by the CF6-80C2 engines for routes from Warsaw to New York, Chicago and Bangkok. Deliveries were scheduled for the second quarter of 1989. Avianca of Colombia ordered two 767-200ERs at the end of 1988 for delivery a year later. PW4000 engines were selected and the aircraft were for the routes to Mexico and the USA.

As well as ILFC keeping their lease stocks available with nine more -300ERs on order, Ansett Worldwide Aviation Services ordered six -300ERs at the end of 1988 as well as some 757s. By the close of the year, Boeing had sold 82 767s in the previous 12 months.

The orders for the 767 continued to be a mix of the small operator and the major trunk carriers topping up as the requirement grew. Amongst the smaller group were Asiana of Korea who ordered two -300s at the beginning of 1989, followed by Aero Maritime, the charter subsidiary of UTA, which ordered two -200ERs and one -300ER in a contract worth about $250 million, the first being delivered in September 1990. Air Algerie ordered three 767-300s worth $264 million for delivery in 1990. Orders from the major carriers included four -300ERs from Varig worth $300 million; sixteen -300s with 16 options in May from United, which selected PW4000 engines; and 10 more -300s in June from All Nippon Airways with 10 further options. This made ANA potentially the world's largest 767 operator with 35 aircraft in service and five more due for delivery before the latest order.

The non-stop long distance point to point records continued to be established, the delivery of the first 767-200ER to Air Seychelles on 27 July 1989 being another example. The twin-jet non-stop distance record of 14,311km was flown from Grand Rapids in Michigan to Mahe in the Indian Ocean.

By the end of September 1989 767 orders had reached 460, of which 276 had been delivered. Evergreen of Taiwan ordered four 767-300ERs the next month for delivery in early 1992. Aer Lingus also decided to acquire two -300ERs for their Shannon-Los Angeles services starting in 1991.

By early 1990 British Airways had received the initial four of its European short haul configuration 767-300s, the first aircraft having been delivered in the previous November. The first Rolls-Royce RB211-524G-powered 767 had rolled out

Right:
Eva Air, part of the Evergreen Group of Taiwan, added a pair of leased 767-300ERs to their order to allow for an early start of operations.

Below:
EI-CAL was one of two 767-300ERs ordered by Aer Lingus for their Shannon-Los Angeles service, starting in 1991.

at Boeing in April 1989, commencing flight testing on 23 May. CAA clearance was given in July and certification was achieved of the 60,600lb-thrust 524H version in November. Following the four European aircraft were four more three-class aircraft for the Middle Eastern routes.

An early problem experienced by British Airways was cracks in the pylons supporting the one ton heavier Rolls-Royce engines, over the competing GE and PW power plants. The cracks, which were up to 33cm long and discovered when removed fasteners could not be replaced, were found in aircraft which had flown between 250 and 1,000 hr. The high time aircraft also had the highest cycles with nearly 1,100 landings on the London-Paris route. The aircraft were grounded for a period from 23 August 1990 while temporary repairs were made, pending a limited redesign to remove the concentration of stresses in the critical area. The problem had obviously been caused by the unique engine installation, the implications of which had not been fully understood. Further repairs were also required a year later.

The first of two 767-200ERs for Royal Brunei Airlines, leased from Ansett International, set new speed and endurance records in June 1990 despite problems with fuel burn guarantees with the PW4056 engines. The aircraft departed Seattle on 8 June loaded with 76.5t of high density JP-5 fuel. After climbing to 37,000ft a maximum endurance cruise speed of Mach 0.77 was selected. The aircraft arrived at Nairobi, having set a great circle distance record of 8,040nm (14,890km), circling Mombasa before landing to increase the distance. The aircraft landed with 2.3t of fuel remaining, equivalent to 30min, allowed because it was a non-revenue flight. In addition to the distance record, a speed record was claimed of 450kt in a journey time of 17hr 22min between Seattle and Nairobi before flying on to Mombasa.

As the end of 1990 approached, the current world economic depression was beginning to make itself felt, accelerated rapidly by the Gulf War. LAM of Mozambique ordered two 767-200s and three 767-300s in August and Air Pacific of Fiji ordered one -300ER in October. Some moves for the future were still being made with Gulf Air adding to their fleet by 12 767-300ERs worth $1.15 billion. EVA of Taiwan leased a pair of -300ERs, in addition to the already two firm and two options, for an early start to daily services to Singapore, Bangkok, Kuala Lumpur and Seoul. At the end of the year Delta ordered six more 767-200s and four 767-300s. Malev became the second East European customer with an order for two 767-200s in February 1991 and Air New Zealand confirmed orders for four more -300ERs in March with five options.

The first major accident to a Boeing 767 happened on 27 May 1991 to a Lauda Air -300ER, 15min after take-off from Bangkok at around 26,000ft. A sudden catastrophic failure killed 223 people on board as it fell into the Thai jungle. Immediate speculation suggested an explosion, maybe caused by sabotage. However, a painstaking investigation, despite the loss of much evidence due to pilfering by the local population, established that the reverse thrust was inadvertently deployed in flight on the port engine. This caused a loss of control which could not be regained.

Having established the cause, the urgent action was to avoid repetition, and following the findings of the full accident enquiry, to establish permanent corrective modifications.

No further sales of the 767 have been announced at the time of writing, with total sales now at 598. The world economy has obviously slowed down new orders, but with a healthy forward order book, and no reported cancellations as yet, the Boeing 767 programme is well established, and ready to pick up new commitments with early deliveries.

6. Boeing 757 Sales and Service Entry

The Boeing 757 was launched into production by a simultaneous selection on 31 August 1978 by British Airways and Eastern Airlines for, respectively, 19 and 21 aircraft with options on 18 and 24. These aircraft had a length of 172ft 9in (52.65m) providing accommodation for 164 mixed-class or a maximum of 195 passengers. Both airlines selected the Rolls-Royce RB211-535 engine, following a long and hard sales campaign.

On 2 March 1979, British Airways confirmed their order, worth $300 million, for 19 Boeing 757s for entry into service starting in 1983 and three months later confirmed their 18 options. Seating was for 12 first-class and 174 economy-class passengers or up to 200 all economy. In addition to the full passenger load, 6,000kg of cargo could also be carried throughout the European network.

The formal launch of the Boeing 757 was made in March 1979, following Eastern Airlines' confirmation of its order for 21 aircraft on 23 March, worth $580 million. Options remained for 24 aircraft, and the order was increased by four aircraft in July 1980, retaining the same number of options.

With the programme now under way, the design was frozen allowing production to commence on the launch order total of 40 aircraft.

It was with some relief when, on 12 November 1980, Delta Airlines and Boeing jointly announced an understanding for the purchase of 60 757-232 aircraft. The purchase was covered by multiple contracts, representing an overall investment by Delta of over $3 billion, with the first delivery in late 1984 and continuing through to 1990.

The Delta aircraft are in a two-class configuration, seating up to 190 passengers, and replace DC-9 and 727 airliners on the medium and short-range routes, flying on such routes as Memphis-Chicago, Seattle-Dallas/Forth Worth, Atlanta-Savannah, Chicago-Cincinnati, Jackson-Atlanta and Boston-Montreal. The Pratt & Whitney 2037 engines were selected by Delta in early 1981. Following tests in September 1987, Delta's 757s were cleared to operate from the noise conscious John Wayne Airport in Orange County, California. Schedules commenced on 1 November to Salt Lake City. Delta increased its options from 10 to 20, with 60 on order and 28 delivered.

In January 1981, American Airlines was reported to have ordered 15 757s plus 15 options, worth $375 million, and powered by the Pratt & Whitney engines. However, McDonnell Douglas eventually won the order for 100 of its Super 80 stretched DC-9.

Below:
Eastern Airlines shared the 757 launch with British Airways. N519EA is seen at Orlando in August 1988; the airline, however, collapsed on 18 January 1991 following protracted union/management and financial problems. *P. J. Birtles*

Top:
In March 1979 British Airways confirmed their initial order for 19 757s as launch customer. BA was followed later the same month by Eastern.
Adrian Meredith/BA

Centre:
Delta became the third airline to order the 757 when 60 aircraft were purchased in November 1980, nearly a year and a half after the aircraft was launched.
Delta

Above:
The Delta 757s replaced DC-9s and 727s on domestic routes, with schedules commencing in November 1980. N607DL is pictured approaching Orlando in August 1988. *P. J. Birtles*

The next positive order was from the Luton-based Monarch Airlines for two 757s on 19 February 1981 to replace its Boeing 720s. Power came from Rolls-Royce engines, as would be expected, and in particular the more economic E4 engine. Although only a modest initial order, as the airline's holiday inclusive tour business expanded so the fleet increased to six aircraft by the 1987 season.

Other frustrated orders included three 757's, with options on three more, powered by the Rolls-Royce engines for Air Florida in August 1981; and Air Malta was reported to have selected one or two 757s the following month to replace its 720, but this was never confirmed.

With the usual Boeing production efficiency, it was found possible to bring the initial delivery schedule ahead to the end of 1982; the first Rolls-Royce engine being installed on the prototype aircraft at the end of October 1981, some two weeks ahead of schedule. The US-type certification for the 757 was achieved on 17 December 1982, about one month ahead of schedule, with British certification following by mid-January 1983. The first 757 was delivered to Eastern on 22 December 1982, allowing services to commence on 1 January 1983 on the Atlanta-Tampa and Atlanta-Miami non-stop services, carrying 148 passengers on the inaugural flight. These services were operated daily and on 16 January were extended to other US cities and to Nassau. Eastern claimed that the 757 was the only air-

Top:
Monarch Airlines of Luton ordered their first two 757s in February 1981. The aircraft were destined to replace Boeing 720s on the airline's charter operations.

Above:
British Airways commenced 757 shuttle services from Heathrow to Belfast on 9 February 1983. Later shuttles to Glasgow, Manchester and Edinburgh were added. G-BIKK is seen landing with a shuttle service at Manchester in January 1989. *P. J. Birtles*

craft, which with all its 185 seats filled, can fly a passenger 700 miles using 10.4 gallons of fuel. In overall fuel economy, the 757 is 50% better than the earlier generation jets which it replaces.

British Airways took delivery of its first 757 on 25 January 1983 ready for the first operation to

Top:
Monarch Airlines leased their 757 G-DRJC to British Airways in the summer of 1988, at which time the aircraft was painted in full BA livery. *P. J. Birtles*

Above:
In July 1982 the Gatwick-based Air Europe placed their start-up order for two 757s. These were initially for charter operations but the airline later developed a European network of scheduled services. However, the airline ceased operations on 8 March 1991 due to financial difficulties. *P. J. Birtles*

commence on the shuttle service from Heathrow to Belfast on 9 February. The Glasgow shuttle was added later the same month; and with three more aircraft delivered in March, the shuttles to Manchester and Edinburgh were added. The aircraft, which replaced Trident 3s, had 189 seats at a 32in pitch in a two-class, Club and Tourist, layout. From the summer of 1983 international routes to Rome, Milan, Paris and Copenhagen were flown by the 757 for the first time, expanding to Athens, Nice, Amsterdam, and Frankfurt in October, and Geneva and Zurich in January 1984. British Airways continued to top up their 757 orders over the years, adding two more in April 1987, three more in August 1987, and one more in late 1988, specifying for the first time the -535E4 engines. A further five -535E4-powered 757s were ordered in October 1990.

In March 1981 Finnair interest in the 757 was prompted by an attractive deal being made to the airline by Pratt & Whitney, but this was not a successful sale for Boeing as the stretched DC-9 was eventually chosen. Lacsa of Costa Rica also

apparently ordered two Rolls-Royce-powered 757s in April 1982, but this $90 million order was not confirmed.

On 2 July 1982 the Gatwick-based charter airline Air Europe placed an order for two 757s powered by the Rolls-Royce -535C engines, which were later upgraded to E4. These two aircraft were part of the British Airways order, allowing Air Europe to achieve early deliveries at an advantageous price. As part of the deal, the two airlines were also to provide a 'swap-lease' involving leasing arrangements on 737s and 757s between them. British Airways would reduce its capital needs by $40 million over two years and supply Air Europe with flight crews, simulator facilities, spares, technical support and probably some maintenance. Air Europe took delivery of its first aircraft, G-BKRM, at Gatwick

on 6 April 1983 and commenced services on 23 April. By this time the 757 fleet as a whole had achieved a 97% reliability with the Rolls-Royce engines performing as specified. While waiting for the second 757 to be delivered in 1984, Air Europe leased a British Airways 757 for the busy summer season. Each aircraft had six crews trained to fly it and initial utilisation was planned at 3,600hr annually. In May 1984, Air Europe increased its fleet of 757s by ordering another aircraft, worth $26 million, scheduled for delivery in March 1985. In mid-1987 five more 757s were ordered for delivery commencing in March 1988, leased from Mercantile Credit. In April 1988 Air Europe placed a major order for 22 -535E4-powered 757s to cover requirements for the next five years, subject to finance.

The first 757 for Monarch Airlines was delivered to Luton on 21 March 1983, painted in the new company livery. The aircraft was fitted with 228 seats at a 29-30in pitch and services commenced on 26 March.

By April, the 757s with Eastern and British Airways had completed three months in service, achieving high reliability and fuel efficiency. The nine aircraft in service had flown 2,190hr from 1 January to 28 March, making 1,330 revenue flights and achieving a 96.3% reliability of departures within 15min of schedule. Eastern's first 757 had flown 585hr by the end of March with 316 revenue departures, and the British Airways aircraft had made 442 landings. Ten of the 123 aircraft ordered to date had been delivered, four each to Eastern and British Airways, and one each to Monarch and Air Europe.

The next order was an unusual one from Singapore Airlines, as four Boeing 757s were selected on 31 May 1983, together with six Air-

bus A310-200s, launching two new types into the Asian market. The Singapore 757s seat 185 passengers and the airline later chose the Pratt & Whitney engines. The first 757 was delivered on 12 November 1984 and was ceremoniously introduced into service at Changi on 1 December, together with the Airbus 310. The 757 was used to serve Kuala Lumpur, Jakarta, Medan, Kuantan and Penang. The Singapore Airlines policy is to maintain a young fleet, the 757s and A310s having been acquired on a one-for-one trade-in of 10 Airbus 300s which were purchased only four years previously. This gave an average fleet age of 27 months and SIA planned to monitor the performance of the two new types closely to decide the basis of any future orders. It was later decided to standardise, at least for the time being, on the Airbus products for the continental and regional routes, SIA returning the 757s to ILFC which supplied them to American Transair with two new aircraft starting in late 1989.

On 25 August 1983, the new Munich-based carrier, Lufttransport-Sud (LTS) ordered two Rolls-Royce RB211-535C-powered 757s, with on option on a third, which was later confirmed. The value of the order was $85 million, and the

aircraft were for charter services from Southern Germany to the Mediterranean and North African resorts. By March 1984, final assembly of the first aircraft was well advanced for the early April roll out at Renton. It was delivered on 25 May and services commenced on 7 June. The airline's name was changed to LTU Sud at the end of 1987 and a new livery was adopted on their fourth aircraft with three more still on order. LTU is in effect a charter group operating two separate German airlines LTU and LTU Sud and has a 25% share holding in the Spanish LTE with a fleet of three 757s.

Meanwhile, in September 1983, after just over seven months in service with British Airways, certification was awarded for Category 3B auto

Above:
Royal Air Maroc placed an order for two 757s for its European and Middle East routes. CN-RMZ is seen on approach to London Heathrow in December 1988.
P. J. Birtles

Right:
Royal Nepal Airlines is the only operator of a 757-200 Combi, which is similar to a passenger aircraft but with the cargo door on the port side of the cabin.

land, the minima being 150m runway visual range and 14ft decision height. Work continued towards Category 3C which was theoretically zero-zero, but in practice a visibility of 75m is maintained for normal operations to allow the crews to taxi the aircraft visually.

After nine months in service, 23 757s had been delivered to the first four operators, flying a total of 25,729hr during 15,260 revenue flights. The despatch reliability was over 97%, with Monarch reporting a cumulative 98.6% reliability with its four aircraft, and actually achieving 100% for a one week period. Monarch averaged 7.2hr/day and one of its aircraft was the lead high time 757 with 2,046 flying hours. One of the British Airways aircraft led on landings with a total of 1,343.

On 29 November 1983, the first significant order for the 757, since the Delta order three years previously, was placed by Northwest Airlines. A total of 20 Pratt & Whitney-powered aircraft with 185 seats in a first-class/tourist layout was initially ordered. In October 1985 a further 10 757-200s were ordered for use on the US transcontinental services with deliveries between 1987 and 1989. The initial order was to supple-ment the existing fleet to allow domestic route expansion, while the later order was to replace some of the airline's 727s. This order arrived in time to maintain a steady production rate, avoiding the possibility of an expensive slow down. By this time, Pratt & Whitney had received contracts for some 250 PW2037 engines to be supplied to Delta, Singapore and Northwest. The first Northwest aircraft was delivered on 28 February 1985, and services commenced from Minneapolis St Paul on 15 March. The final two aircraft were delivered in 1989. In January 1988, however, three further PW2037-powered 757s were ordered capable of carrying up to 184 passengers. In 1986 Northwest acquired Republic to provide a domestic feed for its international operation. The Rolls-Royce-powered Republic 757s were returned to Boeing in exchange for PW-powered aircraft to retain commonality. Their 757s are fitted with ACARS (Arinc Communications and Reporting System) reducing reliance on voice communications for technical matters.

In March 1985 the fourth 757 was delivered to Monarch at Luton, which became the first in Europe to be fitted with the Rolls-Royce

71

RB211-535E4 engine, with the plan being to retrofit the remainder of the fleet. A further aircraft was leased from ILFC and delivered in May 1987, and two more were ordered in April 1988.

After 19 months in service, the reliability of the 757s continued to improve in commercial operation. The 35 twin-jets powered by Rolls-Royce engines had achieved a cumulative despatch reliability of 97.8%, LTS having recorded a short term reliability of 100%. Monarch achieved an overall 98.8% with their three aircraft, while Air Europe maintained the best extended reliability of 99%. Cumulative fleet-wide utilisation averaged 7.1hr/day, with Air Europe's 10hr/day as the highest, followed by LTS with 9.5hr. Over the initial 18 months the fleet flew 83,889hr and made 50,659 revenue departures. Some 36 million miles had been flown, and an estimated 6 million passengers carried in commercial service.

The first customer for the 757-200ER extended range version was Royal Brunei, whose order, worth $175 million, for three Rolls-Royce RB211-535E4-powered aircraft was announced at the Paris Air Show on 30 May 1985. These aircraft would be able to fly from Brunei to Europe with one stop. The aircraft interiors featured a spacious 142-seat, three-class layout of 16 first, 30 business and the remainder tourist seats, with deep carpet, leather covering for the first-class seats and gold-plated fittings in the roomy, well-appointed toilets. The first aircraft was delivered on 6 May 1986 with services commencing soon after.

In the battle with Airbus Industrie to sell 757s to Indian Airlines, Boeing had been close to completing the aircraft when they lost the sale. The Republic Airlines order for six Rolls-Royce

Below:
Air 2000 became the first Manchester-based charter airline for many years when two 757s were ordered in April 1986 for charter operations. The first aircraft, G-OOOA, is about to depart from Manchester in January 1989. *P. J. Birtles*

Bottom:
El Al ordered 757s for its European routes in October 1986 to replace Boeing 707s. 4X-EBR is pictured landing at Manchester in January 1989. *P. J. Birtles*

E4-powered aircraft worth $240 million on 1 October 1985 was, therefore, very welcome and ensured an early delivery. Options were placed for a further six aircraft. The Rolls-Royce engines were selected due to superior reliability and lower ownership costs. This was the second major US airline to choose the Rolls-Royce -535, the requirement being 15 engines worth $84 million for the first six aircraft. The first aircraft, N602RC, was delivered on 6 December 1985, with two more the same month, allowing services to commence in time for the busy Christmas season.

The next order for the standard passenger version was for two 757-200s for Royal Air Maroc, which was announced on 5 February 1986. The Pratt & Whitney PW2037 engine was selected by this first operator in the African/Middle Eastern area, providing a maximum gross take-off weight of 240,000lb. The cabin interior accommodates 20 first-class and 164 tourist seats, the new aircraft replacing B707s on the Middle East routes; Casablanca-Jedda being achieved non-stop. The first 757 for RAM, CN-RMT, set a new distance record for the type on its delivery flight from Seattle to Casablanca in July 1986, when it flew 5,653 miles non-stop. The second aircraft was delivered to the airline the following month.

Royal Nepal Airlines also ordered two 757s in February 1986, one of which was a Combi, both powered by the -535E4 engines. Delivery was made in September 1987.

International Leasing ordered one 757-200 for an unspecified West European airline in April 1986, powered by -535E4 engines and scheduled for delivery in April 1987. On 18 June, this order was confirmed as being one of two 757s for a new Manchester (UK)-based charter airline known as Air 2000. The other aircraft was leased from Chemco Financial Services of New York. The total value of the order was $60 million and Rolls-Royce -535E4 engines were specified. The plan was to start services with both 228-seat aircraft from Manchester in May 1987 for the summer season and then to operate one from Gatwick in the winter. The first aircraft arrived at Manchester on 3 April, followed by the second aircraft by the end of the month, services commencing on 11 April, eventually covering 15 Mediterranean destinations averaging 16hr/day utilisation. Air 2000 began their steady fleet expansion by ordering two more 757s in November 1987 for delivery the following May. Although the airline was nominally Manchester-based, its major operations were from Gatwick, where there is the main operations base, and Glasgow. The second two aircraft were EROPS-capable for winter long-haul operations with one stop to Florida, Mexico, the Caribbean and Asia. By early 1992 the Air 2000 fleet had grown to 15 757s.

Right:
Some 757s were delivered to China in the basic CAAC livery.

Below:
With the reorganisation of commercial aviation in China, additional regional operators were formed; this Shanghai Airlines 757, pictured with a more progressive colour scheme, is an example of this policy.

Bottom:
United placed a substantial order for 30 757s, plus options on a further 30, for delivery between 1989 and 1991. Further orders were placed in April 1989.

In October 1986 El Al ordered three 757s, subject to Israeli Government approval, which was granted a year later. The cabin seats 191 passengers in business and economy-class, replacing 707s on some of the airline's routes to Europe. After lengthy discussions with current 757 operators, Rolls-Royce RB211-535E4s were selected due to their greater efficiency and reliability, despite the fact that El Al had always used Pratt & Whitney engines in the past. The first aircraft was delivered in November 1987, with the second in December.

This brought 757 sales to a total of 193 aircraft over an eight-year period. Although the aircraft has proved successful in service, its impact upon the market place can hardly be described as dramatic at this stage. However, it was not long before sales increased significantly, making the 757 a best seller in worldwide markets. In many cases, the aircraft was used to upgrade from routes developed by the 727 and 737, where additional capacity was required.

In early 1987 the Phoenix-based America West ordered three 757s with options on three more, powered by RB211-535E4s, and in December 1988, the airline ordered 10 more 757s with options on a further 15. Air Holland ordered three 757-200s in July 1987 for delivery in the spring of 1988 for trans-Atlantic charter flights, but they later ceased operations and their aircraft were used by Britannia Airways in the 1991 holiday season, pending the delivery of their own aircraft in 1992.

In October 1987 CAAC of China also ordered three Rolls-Royce-powered 757s with three more one year later. With the reorganisation of commercial aviation in China, CAAC was split into a number of groupings. One example was Shanghai Airlines, which ordered three 757-200s in December 1988, powered by PW2037 engines. The aircraft were allocated initially to domestic routes serving Beijing, Guangzhou and Xion, the first aircraft arriving on 8 August 1989. Shanghai ordered five more 757s in late 1991 powered by PW2000 engines. CAAC continued to co-ordi-

nate some orders, adding 13 757 options in mid-1990 as part of a larger acquisition, and converting these to firm orders in August 1991. With the encouraging interest in the 757, Boeing increased the production rate to four aircraft per month. Orders had now grown to 224 with 137 delivered. Ansett also ordered six 757s with six options which were taken up in July 1988, and continued to add to their lease portfolio with 16 more Rolls-Royce-powered 757s in November 1988, and 10 more in April 1990.

An early order in 1988 was from Caledonian Airways for two 757s with options on six more. These aircraft were specified with RB211-535E4 engines, the total value being around $100 million. In May 1988 ILFC ordered nine 757s, but at the end of the month orders were confirmed for 160 aircraft worth $6.6 billion. The orders came from American Airlines for 50 535E4-powered aircraft with 50 options and 30 orders and 30 options for PW2000-powered 757s for United. The ordered aircraft for United were scheduled for delivery between 1989 and 1991 with the American aircraft due from 1989 through to 1993. The American order was to allow replacement of 727s and some 737s, the low noise of the Rolls-Royce engines being critical. American placed an order for another 16 757-200s in mid-1991. United planned to retire 29 DC-8s, bringing benefits of greater Boeing commonality. In September 1988, Delta added 50 options for 757s in addition to previous orders.

Odyssey International, formed in December 1988, placed an order for three 757-200ERs for regular charter operations from Stansted and Bristol to Toronto. Flights were also made to Manchester, but the airline ceased trading after about two years of operations. An opening order

Below:
The Gatwick-based Caledonian Airways, previously British Airtours, operates a mixed fleet of 757s and TriStars. The airline represents the charter arm of British Airways. One of its 757s, G-APEA, is photographed landing at Luton in April 1992.
P. J. Birtles

for 1989 came from Sterling Airways of Denmark for three -535E4-powered 757s with options on three more. The aircraft in this $150 million order are configured with 219 seats. Air 2000 formed a Canadian associate company, Air 3000, and ordered two 757s for charter flights from Toronto to Florida, the Caribbean and Mexico. This also gave a greater flexibility across the combined fleets.

United Airlines increased their orders for PW-powered 757s in April 1989 with 60 confirmed and another 60 options, giving the order book a significant boost. By the end of the month a $17 billion order was placed by a consortium of GPA and Rolls-Royce including 50 757s. In October, Northwest further increased their 757 orders by 40 aircraft with options on another 40 for delivery between 1993 and 1998. MEA had hoped to buy two 757s to replace their aged 707s for delivery at the end of 1990, but the political and economic environment did not allow this to go ahead in the short term.

Although not affecting the overall order book, Avensa of Venezuela acquired two ex-Air Europe 757s in April 1990, replacing 727s on the Caracas-Miami/New York routes. Icelandair became a new operator when its first 757 was delivered in April 1990 to replace DC-8s on its trans-Atlantic routes, such as Stockholm-Baltimore, with seats for 22 business-class and 167 economy-class passengers.

As part of their restructuring due to reduced profits in mid-1990, Britannia Airways decided to add six 757s by 1992, with four in 1991 on short

Above:
Odyssey International was a Canadian 757 charter operator which survived for about two years on trans-Atlantic charters. C-GTDL, one of its fleet of 757s, is seen about to touch down at Manchester in April 1990. *P. J. Birtles*

Below:
When Odyssey International ceased operations, the newly-formed Nationair Canada took over the routes. Boeing 757 C-GNXI is pictured landing at London Gatwick. *Bruce Malcolm*

Top right:
Air Holland was a 757 charter operator for a short while, but when the airline ceased operations in 1991 the aircraft were taken over by Britannia Airways. One of Air Holland's 757s, PH-AHK, is seen at London Gatwick. *Bruce Malcolm*

Above right:
Prior to receiving its own 757s, Britannia operated two of the ex-Air Holland aircraft. G-OAHK is photographed at Luton in April. This aircraft was previously registered PH-AHK and as such featured in the last photograph. *P. J. Birtles*

Right:
Condor is the charter division of Lufthansa. The airline has nine 757s in service, with nine more on order. D-ABNX is caught landing at Rhodes, a popular holiday destination, in October 1990. *P. J. Birtles*

Below right:
American Trans Air operates a fleet of six 757s, amongst other aircraft, on both scheduled and charter flights. N752AT is seen after landing at Gatwick. *Bruce Malcolm*

term lease. The plan was to reduce overall numbers of aircraft by retiring some of the older maintenance-hungry 737-200s. Britannia decided in August 1991 to acquire a further six 757s; the plan being eventually to replace all the 737s. LADECO of Chile leased two 757s from ILFC in mid-1990 to replace 707s on non-stop services from Santiago to Miami and New York.

Boeing penetrated the Airbus market in June 1990 with an order by Iberia for 16 757s plus options on 12 aircraft, all worth $1 billion. They were configured with 86 business-class and 102 tourist-class seats. Continental Airlines joined the 757 club in October 1990 with orders for 25 aircraft and 25 options for use on the airline's high-density medium/long-haul domestic routes, with expansion on to some international flights. 1990 was rounded off with nine previously unannounced 757s for Delta. This airline added four more 757s in mid-1991, bringing the total commitments to 84 aircraft of this type.

In mid-1990, a specially equipped 757 was used to test the avionics fit for the Lockheed/Boeing/GD YF-22A Advanced Tactical

Fighter ahead of the flight testing of the prototype. Some 32 missions were flown over a period of four months, testing the sensors on targets of opportunity. In August 1990, the first production 757 was used for an initial programme of hybrid laminar flow control (HLFC) system flight trials under contract to NASA. These trials indicated savings of between 5-15% on cruise fuel consumption. The test piece was a 6.7m section of wing leading edge, where boundary layer air was sucked through 19 million laser-drilled holes of

up to 0.0125mm diameter, to reduce turbulent low. The difficult decision was to balance the benefits of fuel saving in the cruise with the additional cost of manufacture. This particular aircraft was also used to test the avionics for the YF-23 Advanced Tactical Fighter, competing with the YF-22A, the eventual winner, and then to test the fly-by-wire flight control system for the Boeing 777.

The Gulf Crisis and the worsening world economic situation made 1991 generally a somewhat negative year with deferred orders and a number of second-hand aircraft becoming available in the marketplace. The first major casualty, which had been terminally ill for some time, was Eastern Airlines. After lengthy operations under the protection of Chapter 11, they finally ceased operations on 18 January, after 64 years in operation. Their aircraft and facilities at Miami, Atlanta and other airports were in many cases just left as they were. Some aircraft were ferried to desert storage, while others were still on the abandoned gates at Atlanta eight months later, with no operators prepared to acquire the assets. Two of the 757s were disposed of, on lease, to Air 2000, arriving at Luton in late 1991 for reconfiguration.

The next casualty was Air Europe which suspended flights on 8 March 1991 with orders still outstanding for 12 757s. As the majority of their aircraft were leased, the 757s were recovered by their owners for reallocation to other operators. On the positive side, Ethiopian Airlines took delivery of the first of five 757s in March 1991.

In November 1991 US Air ordered 15 Rolls-Royce-powered 757s with options on another 15. The airline had already leased 10 of the ex-Eastern 757s, which were reconfigured for entry into service in early 1992; the new aircraft being available from 1993. This brought orders for Rolls-Royce-powered 757s to 403 for 35 operators, which is a major share of the total sales of 770 aircraft by the end of 1991. The Boeing 757 is, therefore, firmly established in world markets and as proof of the original concept, has gone through very little major change since its entry into commercial operations.

7. Boeing 757 Operation

Monarch Airlines of Luton Airport in Britain is a typical inclusive tour charter operator of the Boeing 757. Its major business is the leisure market with each of the aircraft operating out to its destination and back in a day, avoiding costly night stops away from base. The airline sells its seats to over 20 holiday companies.

The airline started at Luton in 1968 with Britannia aircraft on passenger and cargo charter, including transporting race horses, and its furthest destination was Woomera in Australia. It also flew crews for shipping companies. The first 757 arrived in March 1983 to replace a Boeing 720B, the cabin being able to hold 228 tourist-class passengers, six abreast with a single centre-aisle.

The Rolls-Royce RB211-535C engines were selected initially to be replaced by the more economic E4 engines when available. This was a completely new engine using some of the -535C modules and requiring modifications to the pylon taking a total of 14 days to install.

The main maintenance base is at Luton where, out of the first four aircraft, one was based. Two were based at Gatwick where there is also located an engineering base, operations room and cabin staff. A fourth aircraft operated from Manchester. The main spares backup is from the Boeing facility at Reading.

All the major Mediterranean destinations are served, the Greek Islands being particularly popular and the aircraft is capable of reaching Ovda in Israel non-stop. In the winter, the Canaries, Faro, Malaga, Israel and Florida are popular for the warm climates, while Geneva, Munich and Salzburg are used for winter sports. Daily utilisation exceeds nine hours with an average of a one hour turn around at the destination and 1.15hr at base. For the four initial aircraft, G-MONB-G-MONE, 32 captains and 29 first officers were trained.

With Monarch's introduction of the Boeing 757, the major innovation was the flying of the aircraft through computers and the replacement of the traditional analogue primary cockpit instrumentation with digital displays on small cathode ray tubes (CRTs). This electronic flight instrument system (EFIS) includes colour presentations on

the electronic altitude and direction indicator (EADI) replacing the flight director, and the electronic horizontal situation indicator (EHSI) which provides an electronic map display giving track, way-points and routeing information. Two CRT screens in the centre of the main instrument panel provide all the engine parameters including warnings. If a serious fault occurs a red warning is flashed on the screen in addition to the master warning light and an audio signal. A caution is shown by an amber warning, single audio noise and the master caution light. Any advisory information is by green indicators. All the major emergency drills are committed to the computer memory, examples being engine fire, loss of power, rejected take-off, aborted engine start, overspeed and stall. All other actions, whether emergency or routine, are referred to the hard copy quick reference handbook (QRH). The screens which provide the emergency and general operating information are the engine indication and crew alerting system (EICAS). They are programmed to display only necessary information and when working through a check list, progress can only be made when the relevant previous action has been taken. In the unlikely case of a screen failing, the information can be switched to an alternative.

Triplex auto land is fitted to Cat 3B standard allowing a 14ft decision height and 75m runway visual range (RVR) allowing the crew to remain in the decision making process. The take-off of the 757 is done manually to an altitude of 200ft when the vertical pitch mode is engaged. The planned routeing is programmed into the computer

before departure, and the crew follow the indications until 500ft altitude where the auto pilot is engaged to control lateral navigation and the climb rate. Vnav is engaged at the cruise flight level, the flight control computers generating vertical and lateral profiles, feeding them to the auto pilot. The very accurate inertial navigation system positions the aircraft better than air traffic control, the operation being through a pair of Sperry flight management systems (FMS) with a 104,000 computer words data memory growing to 4 million computer words, covering the entire route system. The inertial reference system (IRS) contains laser gyros which feed into the FMS. The actual position is located by three INS positions, refined by the FMS to generate even greater accuracy. The FMS is self tuning to external navigation aids. The maximum cruising altitude at Mach 0.79 is 39,000ft at a weight of 87,000kg.

All major checks, including engines, are carried out at Luton, usually taking two weeks once a year. The maintenance programme consists of a number of checks. Check A is the pre-flight inspection usually done by the flight crew at the destination. Check B is a daily check by the maintenance staff looking at fluids, tyre pressures and other consumable items. The check C is after every 50 flying hours, taking about three hours overnight, checking systems functions and engine condition. Check D is after 400 flying hours or 300 cycles, which takes overnight and consists of more detailed area checks and catching up on any reported snags. The check 2D is similar but is done after 800 flying hours or three months. A check E is carried out after 4,000 flying hours, 3,000 cycles or 15 months. A check F is twice a check E in duration; and the most comprehensive check which can be done progressively is the 12,000-flying hour check G.

The new hangar at Luton has room for two 757s at a time and Monarch continues to undertake third-party maintenance for Boeing 737s and other operators' 757s. The airline tries to be self-sufficient on spares, covering consumable and rotatable components. Major support comes from the conveniently located spares store for Europe at Reading, while direct contact is maintained with the vendors for other parts. There is also good contact between other operators. Many systems are normally returned to the manufacturer under warranty or for specialised over-

Left:
Monarch are a major British charter operator of 757s and are based at Luton. Extended range version G-MONE is seen departing from the airline's home base in March 1992. *P. J. Birtles*

haul, the electronics being one example. Monarch overhauls wheels and brakes, has a limited hydraulic overhaul capability and can undertake airframe repairs. Both Boeing and Rolls-Royce provide technical representatives to assist with engineering liaison.

The flight crew conversion training consists of a four-week course commencing with three weeks of technical training for up to eight complete crews at a time before taking the CAA exam on the aircraft type. This training includes two engineering sessions in the fixed base procedure trainer using the static Boeing 767 simulator. Following the CAA exam are two more fixed base simulator sessions with visual references, but without motion. The final three days are used for company lectures and emergency procedures including smoke drills, ditching drill and an actual slide evacuation.

The crews then have seven days, usually split ideally three days plus four days, on the full flight simulator either with Britannia Airways, British Airways or Boeing. A total simulated flight time of 28hr covering seven sessions of four hours apiece provides the standard for the Form 1179

Top:
Monarch also operates from a number of other major British airports, including Gatwick. G-DAJB lands at Luton on a murky Saturday morning in March 1992.
P. J. Birtles

Above:
During the winter lull of 1988, Air 2000 leased its second 757 to British Airways. G-OOOB is pictured on approach to Heathrow in February 1988.,   *P. J. Birtles*

type rating test, base check and instrument rating. This is then followed by actual flight training on the aircraft.

The trainee crew have to make a take-off with a simulated engine failure between V1 and V2, climb to circuit height, cleaning up the aircraft. They then make a single engine instrument landing system (ILS) approach, with a manual overshoot followed by a circuit and single engine full stop landing. In addition, circuits are made to familiarise with the take-off and landing procedures, to a proficient standard which usually takes up to a maximum of two hours per pilot, but is often done in 1.30-1.40hr. The pilots, either captain or first officer, fly the routes after their line check.

Monarch is therefore very happy with its major policy decision to move from operating second-hand aircraft to the new generation fuel efficient aircraft at the forefront of technology.

Another major British charter operator is the successful Air 2000 which is 76% owned by the Owners Abroad Group. The remaining shares are held by the directors of the airline. About half the airlines seats are taken up by the present group, giving the required feasibility of operation. Air 2000 concentrates on a low cost, but high quality of service, attracting back satisfied customers. It was also intended that in lean years, the parent company would provide a higher portion of seats to Air 2000, ensuring its economic survival and controlled growth. With 231 seats in each aircraft, a total of 150,000 passengers per year are required to fill each Boeing 757. During the peak summer months, each of Air 2000's aircraft fly around 16½hr/day, giving an annual utilisation of 4,500-5,500hr per 757, of which about 3,000hr are flown in the six summer months.

The 757 was chosen for its better seat/mile costs over smaller aircraft such as the 737, but still being of a realistic size from the point of view of selling the majority of the seats. As an example of its flexibility of operation, the 757 can fly from the Greek island of Corfu non-stop to Glasgow without needing full fuel. The runway length at Corfu does not allow a fully laden 737-300 to take-off on the same route with the required full fuel tanks.

Following the first two 757s for Air 2000, the remainder have been EROPS equipped, giving a still-air full payload range increase to about 3,000nm, allowing non-stop long-haul flights to the Caribbean and Asia during the quieter European winter season.

The Monarch-operated Airline Maintenance and Engineering at Luton performs the maintenance on the Air 2000 fleet, each aircraft being scheduled into an 18hr slot every week. Reliability is absolutely essential to maintain passenger satisfaction and loyalty. Air 2000 has seven crews for each of their aircraft, each crew consisting of nine people including cabin attendants.

To maintain costs to an acceptable level, particularly in the initial acquisition of the aircraft, Air 2000 lease their 757s. Being Manchester-based, the airline avoids some of the congestion of the airports in the southeast, while still serving a significant catchment area in the north. However, a great deal of their business has grown out of Glasgow and Gatwick, the latter airport particularly since the demise of Air Europe. This not only left a gap in the market, but also opened up valuable slots. Air 2000 has no immediate plans to enter the scheduled market, even to the holiday destinations to allow carriage of seat-only passengers. This is usually overcome by providing the seat-only passenger with an accommodation voucher which is not taken up. As part of the quality service, Air 2000 supplies their passengers with a high standard of in-flight catering, examples being champagne cocktails, smoked salmon and a roast main course. This is all provided by a friendly and courteous cabin staff, giving the airline an excellent reputation.

Air 2000 managed to make a profit of over £3 million in its first year of operation, the original investment being £1.7 million. With a controlled steady growth, the airline expects to continue operating profitably to the year 2000 and beyond.

Below:
Air 2000 expanded its fleet of 757s to a total of 14 aircraft by the end of 1991; this total including the two ex-Eastern aircraft. G-OOOH, an extended range version, arrives at Rhodes in October 1990 ready to take out some of the last tourists of the season.
P. J. Birtles

8. Boeing 767 Operation

Above:
Britannia Airways was the first European operator of the wide-body 767-200 for its long-range charters. Its first aircraft, G-BKPW, is seen ready for departure from Luton in January 1989. *P. J. Birtles*

Britannia Airways, also based at Luton, were the first British operator of the Boeing 737 and more recently the Boeing 767. The airline flies mainly charter, in particular the inclusive tour business, but has operated limited scheduled services to holiday destinations. It is part of the Thomson Travel Group and receives 50% of its business from its parent organisation, the remainder being sold on the open market. The routes cover all the Mediterranean holiday resorts, as well as North Africa, Moscow, East Africa, Asia, Australia, Florida and the Caribbean.

Britannia's long-term plan is to expand the 767 fleet to market needs, reducing its fleet of 737s as the older aircraft are sold. A total of 14 767s have been ordered, the latest versions having an extended range capability for the long-haul routes and are powered by the General Electric CF6-80A engines. The early aircraft can carry a maximum of 273 passengers on routes up to 3,000 miles in range, including the African tourist resorts. The first four 767s were delivered to the airline in February/March 1984 and in February/March 1985. For the introduction into service, Britannia shared operational experiences with Braathens of Norway who took delivery of the 767 within the same period of time. This continued until Braathens sold their aircraft in mid-1986.

The aircraft are maintained at the Britannia engineering base at Luton with the airframe overhaul being done in-house apart from component overhaul. The 48,000lb-thrust CF6-80A2 engines for the first four aircraft were supported by three spare engines and three basic spare modules. Britannia undertakes module change, but module overhaul is contracted out to the Dutch national airline KLM as part of its CF6 engineering programme.

Britannia operates out of a total of 22 British airports, but not all with the 767s. The majority of the 767 flights are from Manchester and Gatwick where there are line maintenance bases which can cope with up to the basic 300hr checks.

With an average utilisation of over 15hr/day in the summer and between eight and 10hr in the winter, most aircraft achieve two trips in a day with one hour turn-around at origin and destination. With its super quiet engines achieving Stage 3 noise standards, night restrictions on movements are rare.

To ensure a smooth introduction to this early European customer, so far from the manufacturing base, planning started early by forming a dedicated project team to study product support. The acquisition of an advanced technology aircraft required a totally new support concept. Two resident service engineers, one an avionics specialist and the other to look after the airframe, were supplied by Boeing. General Electric also provided a technical representative to advise on engine maintenance for as long as required. New hangar accommodation was constructed capable of taking one 767, as well as smaller aircraft, and this has now been further expanded as the fleet has grown.

When Britannia was considering new equipment, it studied the Airbus A310, Boeing 757 and 767. The latter offered definite operational advantages to the airline, climbing out quickly above peak traffic and giving a good start during busy times. The 767 with its twin-aisle, 2-4-2 seat, wide-body interior had better passenger appeal. The large galleys are located fore and aft and four toilets are positioned centrally. Free headsets are supplied to the passengers for the music and video system, the latter being used for the safety brief. Flight performance details such as speed, altitude and time to destination are given in a digital display panel. The specially developed seats for the 767 supplied by Avio

Interiors of Italy give greater comfort and leg room in a 30-31in pitch.

In conjunction with Braathens, Britannia designed its own galleys, taking two years to finalise the detail and choose a supplier. The reliable and practical design specification was sold to Ethiopian Airlines.

No freight is carried due to operating licence conditions, but passenger baggage is packed in LD-3 containers which are stacked in the underfloor freight hold, leaving space for bulk loading alongside. The forward hold contains a pair of full width LD-8 containers left on board to cater for bulky loads, particularly winter sports equipment.

For the first four aircraft, crew availability consisted of 32 captains and 30 first officers. Pilot training is on the Redifusion full-flight simulator, initially operated jointly with Braathens, covering close to full conversion standards.

Britannia, with other early users, provided Boeing with in-service data to improve reliability. The initial Britannia 767 made 1,352 revenue departures in the first year with an average utilisation of 9.30hr/day. Despatch reliability was 99.4% with an average annual load factor of 87%, peaking at 95% during August and September. A total of 290,000 passengers were carried on one aircraft in the first year.

Spares provisioning was established, using Boeing mathematical models covering the anticipated operations, combined with Britannia's own value judgment. Limited vital spares were bought from the Boeing store at Reading, and the airline undertakes its own avionics servicing with the relevant automatic test equipment for test and

Below:
Amongst its fleet of 10 767s, Britannia has seven extended range versions. G-BPFV is one of these; it is pictured here at Gatwick in March 1992 ready for departure. *P. J. Birtles*

repair. The airline has a small design office for repairs and modifications, based on the technical manuals, and submits the drawings to Boeing when necessary.

The maintenance consists initially of a basic A check at 300 flying hours, The C check, taking three days to complete, is made annually limited to 2,500hr. An equalised maintenance check (EMC) is carried out after 400 flying hours every four to five weeks, covering the A check items over the year. The structures element is covered on each C check, being fully checked every 3,000 cycles or 15 months. There is no major check as such, all elements being covered in eight C checks. C checks are planned to coincide with the beginning and end of the peak seasons.

The engines are maintained 'on condition', utilising on board airborne integrated data system (AIDS). This automatically records engine and airframe parameters in stable cruise conditions using an on board computer. The resulting data is fed into the base workshop computer to determine engine health. Engine parameters recorded include fan speed (N1), core speed (N2), exhaust gas temperature (EGT), fuel flow in lb/hr, oil temperature and quantity, and any vibration on fan and core. Recorded at the same time are the flight parameters including airspeed, Mach number and all the flight control positions. This data is retained and called off at the end of each trip.

Most of the airframe components are also 'on condition', and as the aircraft become older, greater maintenance down time is required. Corrosion protection has improved since the early 737s were delivered to the airline, by enamel painting of the skins before jointing, avoiding fluid traps and the use of composites such as Kevlar, carbon fibre and glass fibre on secondary structure and control surfaces.

The EICAS alerts to flight defects and interrogates through built-in test equipment (BITE) to determine which line replaceable unit (LRU) to change. The BITE is working well and is self checking.

AIDS, a British system, has a built-in extension to link with ACARS (Airborne Communications Automatic Recording System), the European equivalent. AIRCOM (Air Communications) allows a VHF communications link for the data to be transferred to a digital format via telex to the home base. This avoids delays in waiting for the report and cuts out transcription errors. The aircraft receives a real time health monitoring in flight, with the flight crew reporting back on the fault code for diagnosis and replacement of parts.

Britannia has, therefore, adapted easily to this new generation, high-technology airliner, with its wide-bodied cabin comfort and quiet fuel-efficient engines giving a very much larger range than with the Boeing 737s, and providing complementary operations with the new 757s as they enter service.

In direct contrast to the Britannia Airways charter operations in the UK, Royal Brunei are building up their own brand of high quality scheduled operations based almost exactly in the middle of the world's fastest economic growth area. The government-owned Royal Brunei was formed in November 1974 and operated its first scheduled regional flight in May 1975. The initial fleet was a pair of 737-200s bought new from Boeing. A third 737-200 was added in 1980.

The first of the three 757-200s was introduced in 1986 to operate longer haul routes to Darwin, Taipei and Dubai in addition to the higher capacity regional services to Singapore, Hong Kong, Kuala Lumpur, Bangkok and Jakarta. The 737s were phased out and sold as the 757s arrived.

However, according to the Sultan of Brunei who has almost limitless reserves in oil wealth, he would like the airline to become much more international. The main difficulty is negotiating traffic rights as the small state of Brunei, with a population of less than 230,000 people, does not have a great deal to attract other international airlines.

Royal Brunei, therefore, decided to add the Boeing 767 to their fleet for the long-haul operations, a -200ER being acquired in June 1990, at short notice, on lease from Ansett Worldwide. On an initial enquiry to Boeing in early 1990, no 767 was available soon enough, but Ansett had the two ex-Olympic aircraft on their books with the first one being available within the time scale. This left a major task for the airline of preparing and training the operational and maintenance staff in only three months. The common type rat-

ings of the flight crews helped on the operational side, but the engineering preparation was complicated by the Pratt & Whitney engines on the 767 compared with the Rolls Royce powered 757s. Spares could have been a problem in the time scale, but fortunately Olympic had ordered a complete package which Royal Brunei bought separately.

The 767 started operations on the annual 'Haj' charters, flying Muslim pilgrims from their journey to Mecca. Following this, it was used on regional services in southeast Asia prior to the removal of the Olympic Airways two-class interior. The 767 was then reconfigured with a 167-seat interior (15 first-class, 32 business-class and 120 economy) to the same high standards as the 757s. The seat pitch in economy is 107cm, the seats are leather covered and the toilet fittings in first-class are gold plated.

On completion of its refit, the 767-200ER was introduced on the Brunei-Frankfurt/London routes, and was joined towards the end of 1991 by the larger -300ER. This aircraft was ordered directly off the Boeing production line to RBA's specification with 203 seats (17 first-class, 36 business-class, and 150 economy). Both aircraft are capable of extended range operations, but will have to operate the airframe/engine combi-

nation for at least a year to build up sufficient experience for CAA EROPS approval.

There should not be any problems gaining this approval, as technical cancellations are non-existent and in-flight engine shutdowns are rare. The operations are generally out and back allowing snags to be cleared rapidly, and the high level of preventive maintenance keeps the aircraft serviceable. Due to its isolation the airline has to be self-sufficient in engineering, the maintenance staff totalling about 350 of whom 50 are senior expatriate engineers. A local technical college offers suitable training courses to provide a steady flow of new engineers who serve apprenticeships with Britannia Airways or Aer Lingus before gaining their licences. All the heavy base maintenance is split between C checks — the D check no longer being a valid concept — and the engine shop can do hot-section inspections on the PW JT-8Ds used to power 737s and module breakdown for the RB211s on the 757s.

Initial passenger loads to Europe were disappointingly low even with fifth freedom rights in Bangkok and Dubai allowing the pick up of additional passengers. The intention is to expand the European services to such destinations as Paris, Brussels or Amsterdam once a week to fill in between the London and Frankfurt services. There are also plans to extend its operations in Australia, as well as new services to Japan and Korea. The airline is therefore determined to consolidate and continue its expansion as a truly international flag carrier with the ambition of operating a daily service to Europe, and attracting hub operations around Bandar, the capital of Brunei.

Below:
Royal Brunei 767-300ER, V8-RBF, departs from the Boeing ramp on delivery.

9. The Engines

The General Electric CF6-80A engines were used to power the earlier 767s. *GE*

All three major Western World engine manufacturers shared in the Boeing 757 and 767 power plant programmes, with Pratt & Whitney and Rolls-Royce participating in both aircraft and General Electric offering engines for the 767.

The General Electric CF6-80A and the more recent -80C2 have been developed from the well-proven CF6 family of two shaft turbofans based on the TF39 core. The CF6 was used initially to power the McDonnell Douglas DC-10, later becoming a major engine in the Airbus A300 programme and eventually sharing the Boeing 747 with Pratt & Whitney and Rolls-Royce. The CF6-80A is rated at 48,000lb thrust with a considerable built-in growth potential. The -80A offers better fuel burn and significantly lower maintenance costs than the -50 from which it was developed. The newer engine is 300-400lb lighter than the earlier one depending upon gearbox installations and is 16in shorter due to the elimination of the turbine mid-frame and redesign of the compressor rear-frame and

combustor. The specific fuel consumption at average cruise altitude is improved by six percent, with this 4.7 bypass ratio engine. New standards of inflight reliability have been achieved and the continuing programme of product improvement has produced a significant lowering of direct maintenance costs.

The CF6-80C2, selected by Varig, Piedmont and All Nippon Airways (the latter for its stretched 767-300s), is a further major improvement of the well proven basic CF6 engine. It is designed to give the highest possible reliability, the longest life and the lowest fuel burn. The test bed running of this engine started in March 1984 and it achieved its design capability of 62,500lb of thrust on its first run. New technology of this 5.15 bypass ratio engine includes advance flow

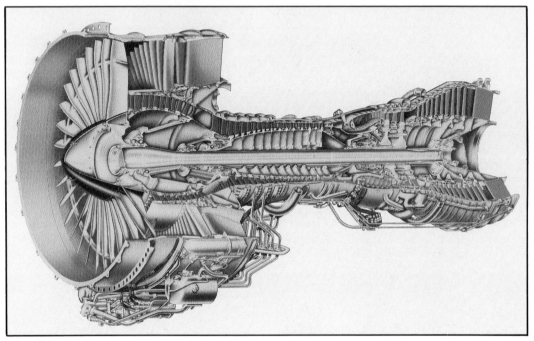

path contouring to reduce pressure losses and refined cooling techniques to improve overall efficiency. The weight has been reduced by casting the titanium fan frame and the turbine rear frame each in one piece. Flight testing of this new variant was from August to December 1984 with certification in June 1985. The -80C can be supplied as a total propulsion system including engine, nacelle and exhaust to maintain a consistent standard of performance and profitability. General Electric has been joined in this programme by Fiat, MTU, Rolls-Royce, SNECMA and Volvo Flygmotor.

The competing Pratt & Whitney JT9D-7R4 engine, first introduced in the late 1970s, is part of a series of engines producing between 38,000

Top left:
The improved GE CF6-80C2 engines are currently used to power some of the extended range and stretched -300 versions of the 767. *GE*

Top right:
The Pratt & Whitney PW2037 turbofan was a direct competitor for the Rolls-Royce RB211 engines in the 757. *P&W*

Above:
Pratt & Whitney PW2000 turbofan cutaway. *Pratt & Whitney*

and 56,000lb thrust. A new wide-chord, single-shroud fan, single-crystal material turbine blades and an electronic engine control, combined with component refinements, give fuel savings of up to eight percent over the earlier -7A engine. The -7R4 engine is achieving the excellent reliability of 0.1 per thousand flying hours. As with the CF6 engine, Pratt & Whitney has developed a nacelle system designed for low weight, minimum drag and ease of maintenance. The -7R4 engines for the Boeing 767 which delivers 48,000lb of thrust was certificated in October 1980 and entered service in September 1982. It was the first engine certificated by the US Federal Aviation Administration (FAA) for extended range operations of up to two hours flying from an alternate airport on transoceanic flights, which is discussed further in the next chapter. The PW4000 engine was developed for later 767s, the 56,000lb-thrust engine making its first flight in April 1987. Lauda Air was the first customer for this engine on its ultra long-haul routes to Asia. A

Right:
The Pratt & Whitney JT9D-7R4 engine was used to power the earlier versions of the 767.

Below
Pratt & Whitney JT9D-7R4 turbofan cutaway.
Both Pratt & Whitney

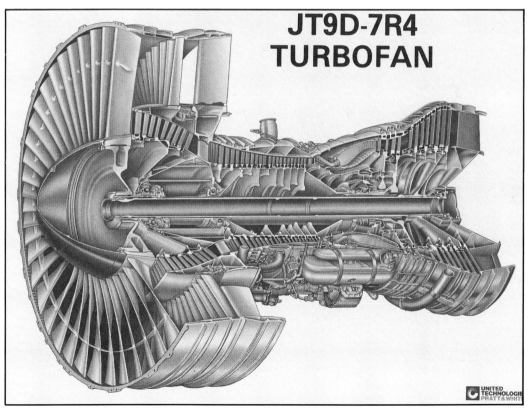

refinement to the PW4000 was the 56,750lb-thrust PW4056 first specified for Air Zimbabwe in August 1988, and also selected by Royal Brunei.

The Pratt & Whitney PW2037, previously known as the JT10D, is a two shaft turbofan launched with an order from Delta in December 1980 for 60 Boeing 757s. It was the only completely new commercial turbofan in production, the other manufacturers offering derivative engines. Development of the PW2037 started in February 1972 for a 26,700lb-thrust engine which first ran on the test bed in August 1974. Rolls-Royce had a 34% share initially, but in the changing market, withdrew to concentrate on its own products. The engine is now produced in collaboration with MTU which has an 11.2% share and Fiat which has four percent. They joined this project as partners in July 1977.

The PW2037 has now become a very fuel efficient, high technology engine developing 37,000lb thrust, running for the first time in December 1981 in its production form on the test bed. Pre-certification testing involved 11 engines in a 5,500hr running time, followed by another 5,000hr after certification and before entry into commercial service.

To increase high-pressure compressor efficiency, the core rotational speeds were increased significantly by driving a smaller compressor much faster. This gave lighter weight and smaller frontal area, but the higher rim

Above:
The Pratt & Whitney 4000 series was used to power the later extended range versions of the 767. *P&W*

Below:
PW4000 turbofan cutaway. *Pratt & Whitney*

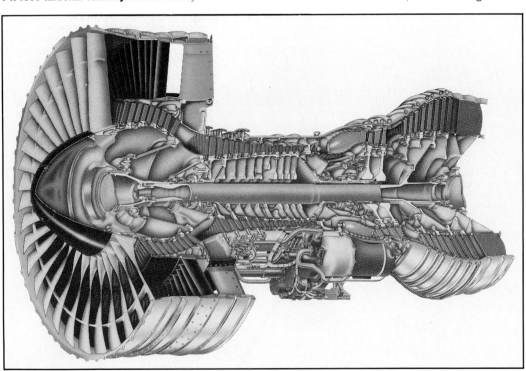

speeds increased the centrifugal loads on the disc to blade attachments. The modular construction allows easy maintenance by replacement of modules, and most of the rotating parts can be inspected with the engine installed on the aircraft.

Flight testing commenced on Pratt & Whitney's test bed Boeing 747 in February 1983, with the first six engines for the 757 flight testing delivered by the end of the year, and production reaching 20-30 engines per month. The first 757, the Boeing prototype, was fitted with PW2037s in March 1984 to achieve certification by October, and service entry with Delta in December. The current production engine develops a thrust of 37,600lb for take-off and has a bypass ratio of 5.8. The engine is certificated to 39,000lb thrust and with development is capable of growth to 45,000lb. By April 1986, the PW2037 engine fleet had flown over 110,000 revenue service flight hours, with the high time engine exceeding 3,000hr. To ensure successful commercial operations, Pratt & Whitney continue to run a PW2037 on endurance testing which they call the Pacer Programme, keeping two years ahead of the airline fleet in terms of hours and cycles. A further development of this engine is the 41,700lb-thrust PW2040 which was first selected by UPS for the 757PF to lift the higher gross weight of 250,000lb.

The Rolls-Royce RB211-535 is a cropped-fan, three-shaft derivative of the larger 42,000lb-thrust -22B used as power plants for the wide bodied jets. Design of the -535 engine was started in February 1977 with the test bench running commencing in April of 1979. By early February 1980, five test engines had completed 700hr of bench running, including 1,500 simulated flight cycles. Only minor problems, which were easily rectified, were encountered, mainly due to the large commonality with the earlier RB211 engine. Both engines share the same high pressure module which has the highest technical risk, allowing any -22B modification to be easily incorporated in the 535. The commonality of the engines also helps with spares and maintenance.

Rolls-Royce planned 3,000hr of test bench running to achieve certification by the spring of 1981 and a further 4,000hr prior to service entry in early 1983. This intensive pre-service testing gave a highly reliable engine from the start of commercial operations.

The initial power rating of the -535 engine was 37,400lb maximum take-off thrust, which gave an adequate margin for normal sea level temperate operations and did not overload the engines for operations from hot and high airfields.

To maintain the highest efficiency Rolls-Royce was responsible for the complete power plant, including engine, accessories and nacelle. The pod makes extensive use of composites to save weight.

Ten days after the roll out of the first Boeing 757, the RB211-535C engines were run on 23 January 1982 for the first time on the aircraft. The following day full power runs and trim tests were carried out, followed on the next day by calibration checks, fuel flow measurement, acceleration responses and checks to the engine's electronic control system.

The next major development by Rolls-Royce was the RB211-535E4 engine developing 40,100lb maximum take-off thrust and an eight percent fuel saving in the cruise. Major changes include the use of wide chord fan blades for greater efficiency; a pressure ratio increase for the high pressure module; and a common exhaust nozzle for the fan and core streams. The higher efficiency core engine of the E4 has an increased pressure ratio of 27:1 as compared with 23:1 on the -535C, contributing to a three percent improvement in the fuel consumption. Since, on the average short-haul flight, about half

Right:
The Rolls-Royce RB211-535C engine was used on the early 757s supplied to British Airways and Eastern. *Rolls-Royce*

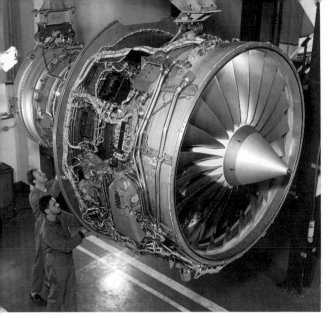

Left:
The Rolls-Royce RB211-535E4 engine became the major 757 powerplant, superseding the original -535C. *Rolls-Royce*

Bottom:
British Airways placed an order for 767-300s when Boeing adopted the Rolls-Royce RB 211-524 G/H as an alternative power plant. *Rolls-Royce*

When British Airways was evaluating the 767, it wanted commonality of supplier of the airframe and engines, as well as flight decks. Rolls-Royce considered the RB211-524D4D engine with a similarity to the current Boeing 747s, but in September 1988, the RB211-524I was unveiled at the Farnborough Show for the newer generation 747s and 767s. Initial thrust was estimated at 63,000lb with even better fuel economy than the -524G. The -524L was a further improvement to 65,000lb growing to 72,000lb. As well as growth in thrust, economy of fuel burn would improve due to revised nacelle aerodynamics and improved fan efficiency.

of the aircraft's fuel is used in climb power, the 11% savings in fuel consumption brought about with the E4 represent a major economy.

The RB211-535E4 engine achieved its type certificate on 30 November 1983 and first flew in the Boeing-owned 757 prototype in February 1984, at the same time as a partnership deal was signed providing General Electric with a 15-25% share in the engine. The 42,500lb-thrust -535E4B was certificated for the Boeing 757 at the end of 1988.

The first BA 767-300 flew with interim -524H engines in June 1989, this being the first time a 767 was powered by Rolls-Royce engines. The test programme took 235hr of flight time, the engines each developing 60,600lb thrust. The production standard engine was flown on 31 August 1989, to complete around 110hr before the first 767-300 was delivered to British Airways in November.

10. Oceanic Twins

Modern fan jet engines have built up an unrivalled reputation for reliability, especially when compared with the earlier piston-engines. Between the wars it was not uncommon for aircraft to have to force land due to engine trouble, and many were powered with three or four engines to allow for an 'in-flight spare' to maintain power in the event of the inevitable failure.

Following World War 2, which had forced forward aircraft technology, regular trans-Atlantic and trans-Pacific commercial flights became feasible. However, because of continuing piston-engined unreliability, although much improved from the 1930s, the US Federal Airworthiness Authority issued in 1953 FAR Part 121.161. This rule stipulates that 'unless authorised to do so by the administration on the basis of the nature of the terrain, the type of operation or the performance of the aircraft involved, no holder of a transport licence shall operate a twin-engined aircraft on a route which at any point lies more than one hour flight, in zero wind and at normal single-engined cruising speed, from an adequate airport'. Although this rule theoretically applies only to US-registered aircraft, its influence in practice is on a much wider scale, affecting most of the operators of US-built or US-operated airliners.

However, the deregulation of US airlines and increased fuel costs caused airlines to look for the most economic aircraft available. The use of twin-engined airliners on routes which offer fewer passengers saves flying the high capacity Boeing 747 and the large trijets with an unacceptable number of empty seats. For example, the cost of operating a Boeing 747 with 370 passengers from St Louis to Paris is $56,000, while that of a Boeing 767 twin on the same route carrying up to 190 passengers is $30,000. This 46% reduction keeps the cost per passenger virtually constant, but the real saving is that a 747 burns 11,400 litres of fuel per hour, compared with 4,900 litres per hour by the 767. Another saving is that the 767 is operated by two crew, while the 747, DC-10 and TriStar all require three flight crew.

Technology has advanced considerably from the 1950s when, according to Boeing calculations, with a fleet of 200 piston-engined airliners of the type in service in 1953, one could expect to suffer a double engine failure once every 16 years. The likelihood of such an event occurring in a fleet of 200 767s has fallen to one in every 40,000 years, assuming the annual utilisation of each aircraft is 2,500hr. Engine reliability has increased to such an extent that any failure was more likely to be due to an associated system, crew miss-selection or spurious warning. Efforts had to be made therefore to improve the reliability of the ancillary systems.

With the economy and therefore increased endurance of the modern twin-jet, the aircraft were adapted for longer routes initially over land. However, the airliner does not know whether it is flying over land or water. With the FAA 60min rule, the 767 could divert typically 400nm, but Boeing was keen to demonstrate that the 767 was a completely reliable long-range twin, the

Below:
Monarch has been using the extended range capability of the 757 for some years, particularly on the North Atlantic route to Orlando, with Bangor in Maine as a technical stop. *P. J. Birtles*

first tests being conducted under the conditions of the 60min rule.

Trans World Airlines ordered 10 767s in December 1979 with the maximum possible fuel capacity, including a wing centre-section fuel tank to allow for its use on long-range routes. In 1983 TWA flew the first non-stop US transcontinental service, demonstrating successfully the required performance in terms of range and navigational accuracy. To confirm these results, Boeing made a demonstration non-stop flight from Lisbon to Seattle, followed by TWA inaugurating

scheduled 767 non-stop flights from the USA to Europe.

The 60min rule did, however, make it impossible to achieve optimum economy on the trans-Atlantic routes, TWA requesting authority to apply the 90min advisory rule so defined by ICAO which gave on average a 690nm single-engined diversion to a suitable airfield.

In due course, the airline received the authorisation but had to modify five of its aircraft with the collaboration of Boeing at a cost of $3 million per aircraft. The consideration here was not just the failure rate of one of the two engines, but the remaining engine would have to work harder to maintain flight, and the reason for the initial failure or shut down may cause additional hazards or difficulty for the operating crew.

In addition, systems integrity had to be taken into account. The remaining single engine-driven generator or hydraulic pump could be subject to overload, and the twin-jet systems integrity has to be as high as that of a multi-engined aircraft. The life expectancy of, for example, an electrical generator is significantly diminished from the

Below:
With Pan-Am and TWA pulling out of the trans-Atlantic routes, United began operation into London Heathrow from North America in 1991. United 767-200ER N607UA is seen at Heathrow in June 1991. *P. J. Birtles*

Bottom:
American Airlines had been operating extended range flights to Manchester in the UK for a number of years, but started regular services to London Heathrow during 1991. Boeing 767-200ER N312AA is ready for departure from runway 27L in March 1992. *P. J. Birtles*

Above:
American Airlines operated both 767-200ERs and -300ERs into London Heathrow, where they joined United in taking over the ex-Pan-Am and TWA North Atlantic routes. N360AA is on finals to Heathrow in April 1992. *P. J. Birtles*

moment it starts to carry the loads alone, requiring an assessment of its failure rate under the more demanding conditions. It is not sufficient to rely on the auxiliary power unit which may or may not start after a cold soak at altitude, battery power which may not last all the way to a diversionary landing, or the emergency ram-air turbine which windmills in the airflow to provide essential power. Obviously the allowable deficiencies on departure are much reduced in the more stringent conditions of long-range flights, and an acceptable diversionary airport needs a runway of at least 8,000ft and suitable landing aids to cater for bad weather.

TWA, therefore, included amongst its modifications an additional 5kVa hydraulically-driven generator, a fire detection and extinguishing system in the underfloor cargo areas, a higher capacity avionics cooling system, additional HF radio and extra life rafts for over ocean operations. A third crew member is carried on the flightdeck whenever the duration is more than eight hours, whether over land or water.

On 28 April 1985, TWA inaugurated scheduled twin-engined trans-Atlantic passenger-carrying services between St Louis and Paris applying the new FAA 120min rule, which allows a maximum diversion distance of 800nm. This rule also takes account of the additional equipment which must be fitted for these flights. TWA then operated trans-Atlantic routes with the 767, under the auspices of the 120min rule and have been joined by American Airlines, Air Canada (in April 1985) and El Al — all operating 767s from the USA to Europe — and Qantas, which operates a number of long-range routes from Sydney and Melbourne. Boeing would like to see a regulation without any diversion time limit, but airlines such as TWA are generally happy with the 120min rule as it does not involve them in any major restrictions. In five months, TWA flew 1,500 trans-Atlantic crossings, building up to 16 crossings a day with 767s. Only four times in the initial five months did the airline have to divert, three times

for compressor stalling and once for a false oil contents indication. On each occasion, the aircraft reached its designated diversion on one engine without drama, and the aircraft was able to depart after inspection without any repair being necessary.

It was, in fact, El Al who pioneered trans-Atlantic operations with Boeing 767s in March 1984 when they flew Montreal to Tel Aviv in 11hr 8min non-stop. During the summer season of 1985 Air Canada operated more than 200 north Atlantic crossings from Halifax to Prestwick and London, within the 60min rule, replacing TriStars, with no diversions, engine shut-downs or power emergencies. Between December 1983 and the end of 1985, Air Canada had operated more than 600 twin-engined overwater flights, starting between Canada and the Caribbean. A diversion time of 138min is allowed on 767s equipped with a fourth generator and extra fire protection, the longest sector being 2,275nm from Toronto to Port of Spain. The minimum requirement is for three serviceable generators and a serviceable APU. The extended range twin-jet operations (ETOPS) systems integrity was tested by Air Canada on the initial delivery flight from Seattle to Montreal, when the APU was started at 41,000ft after a cold soak and was used to power various electrical systems. The main electrical power sources were deliberately interrupted, the ER generator picking up the essential loads, which, combined with the APU, gave the desired protection.

Qantas joined ETOPS operators with flights across the South Pacific and Tasman Sea, the longest being 3,870nm, Brisbane-Tokyo, with a maximum diversion time of 104min. Air New

Zealand also fly 767 ER operations across the Tasman Sea and other routes, and American Airlines commenced 767 ER flights from Chicago to Geneva and Zurich on 1 April 1986. This was followed by links from Dallas/Forth Worth to Frankfurt and London using American Airlines 767-200ERs.

As the market was developing, there also began a need for extended range operations for the Boeing 757, particularly on North Atlantic winter holiday charters.

The Rolls-Royce RB211-535E4 engine on the 757 was cleared by the FAA for 120min ETOPS in December 1986 and was the first engine approved by the FAA for 180min ETOPS in mid-1990. Pratt & Whitney gained FAA certification in April 1990 for 120min ETOPS operations for the PW4000-powered 767s, followed soon after by 180min ETOPS for the earlier JT9D-7R4 engine.

By mid-1988 nearly 100 ETOPS-equipped 767s were in operation with 17 operators on more than 1,500 flights per month. This amounted to 32,000 extended range trips of which 52 had to turn back or had safely diverted. The FAA requires that before considering an engine type for ETOPS operations, it should have accumulated a fleet total of 250,000hr in the air, of which 75,000 must be on the specific airframe for which the approval is requested. The GE CF6-80C2-powered 767s achieved this target in May 1988 gaining FAA approval for 120min ETOPS flights. The engine had demonstrated a very high reliability with an inflight shutdown rate of 0.009 per 1,000 flying hours, with only four inflight shutdowns. Boeing continued to work with Pratt & Whitney to gain approval for the 767/PW4000 and the 757/PW2037 combinations, having achieved it on all the others.

The next step was to move to the 180min rule, most likely to be approved initially with the 767/CF6-80C2 combination, but still the subject of much criticism. Three hours at single engine

Qantas needed the extended range capability of the 767-200 from an early stage. The airline's longest route is 3,870nm from Brisbane to Tokyo.

speed from a suitable diversionary airfield concerned people who believed that running one engine at maximum continuous thrust for a long period must overload it and reduce reliability. Boeing's answer is that the engine temperatures and stresses are far higher on take-off and climb than a long slow cruise following an engine shutdown. The 180min rule would allow more direct fuel saving on southerly routes across the North Atlantic, and the Pacific would be opened up to extended range twin-jet operations. In 1988 some 40% of 767 ER operations were trans-Atlantic, while 50% had been accumulated by Qantas and Air New Zealand mainly across the Tasman Sea separating Australia and New Zealand.

In early 1989 American Airlines was working with the FAA towards approval for the operation of GE-powered 767-300ERs on the Dallas-Hawaii route. This would be the first time the 120min rule would be exceeded and followed a programme of validation flights under FAA observation to give clearance under the 180min rule. This would allow twin-engined airliners to fly up to 1,200nm from the nearest airport, which effectively covered almost all worldwide routes, which was particularly significant across the Pacific Ocean.

In the European environment there was less priority to adopt the 180min rule, because with the 120min rule there were few 'no go' areas across the Atlantic. However, the UK CAA cleared Air Europe and Monarch to operate to the 138min rule (a 15% increase over 120min) which eliminated the last small 'no go' triangle from the North Atlantic. Any restriction requiring 180min would be on direct flights from Europe to Brazil or northern Africa to Central America, but, generally, these routes require landings for commercial reasons and, therefore, did not cause a problem. Before granting 120min dispensation, the CAA insist that the engine type must have a shut down rate of less than 0.05 per 1000 flights, with work being done to improve to 0.03 per 1000. To achieve 180min operations better than 0.02 shutdowns per 1000 flights would need to be demonstrated.

In early 1989 the term ETOPS (extended range twin engined operations) was replaced by the new EROPS (extended range operations). The reasoning was that all long-range airliners should have the same high reliability and safety standards, regardless of the number of engines. This is particularly true for items such as cargo hold fire detection, suppression and containment.

In September 1989 the Rolls-Royce RB211-535E4 and C engines as fitted to the Boeing 757 gained UK CAA approval for 180min of single engined operation. FAA approval was anticipated by the end of the year, which would help American Airlines on their Pacific routes. In-flight shutdown rates on the -535E4 engines over a 12-month period were at the rate of 0.018 per 1,000 engine flight hours. Preparations were also in hand to gain approval for the RB211-524G/H engines fitted to the BA 767-300s. CAA clearance for 120min EROPS was expected in 1991.

Pratt & Whitney gained 120min EROPS certification with the PW2000/Boeing 757 combination in January 1990, with 180min planned by the end of the year. The 270 PW2000-series engines in service up to the time of the 120min approval had built up 1.54 million flight hours and achieved a shutdown rate of 0.03 per 1,000 hours over the previous two years. The larger PW4000 engines had flown 300,000hr service on 150 engines, achieving a shutdown rate of between 0.02 and 0.03 per 1,000 hours.

In April 1991 the FAA gave 120min clearance to the Rolls-Royce RB211-524H/G/767-300 combination, which had achieved no shutdown or unscheduled removals over more than half a million flight hours. As British Airways is the only operator of the combination, they also applied for CAA approval, allowing 120min EROPS to New York to be operational by 1992.

With the 180min rule being achieved on the existing fleet, Boeing was working hard to achieve the same standard on the all new 777 on its entry into service. This is discussed in the next chapter.

Below:
With New Zealand so distant from other major continents, Air New Zealand required extended range operations with their 767-200s, particularly across the Tasman Sea and around Asia.

11. The Boeing 777

Boeing had looked at the type 777 as a trijet variant of the 767, as mentioned earlier, but this programme had been shelved. However, by the late summer of 1988, Boeing was beginning to make public its thoughts on a further 767 development. One suggested route was a modest fuselage stretch of 33in over the existing 767-300, but with a new long-range wing, and the other was a 767-300 with a total of 539in fuselage stretch and the new wing. This latter aircraft was almost as large as a 747-300 in overall dimensions, but powered by only two of the Rolls-Royce RB211-524G or H engines. Despite the longer aircraft carrying up to 150 more passenger than the 261-290 in the -300, it could still be powered by essentially the same engines, although in an exceptional case the newer 524L could be used.

The modest stretch with the new long-range wing, known as the 767RW-300, was targeted for domestic US routes, the North Atlantic and the long, thin Pacific routes. The major stretch known as the 767RW stretch would be able to carry up to 400 passengers and, over ranges of about 5,000nm, 275 passengers. The 767RW-300 would have a range of 7,500nm carrying 206 passengers.

Boeing claimed the Boeing 777 programme was customer-driven from a very early stage. During 1988, it formed a group of eight prospective customer airlines covering the widest geographic area. In the USA, United, American and Delta were represented, with British Airways in Europe (the only major non-Airbus operator) and Qantas, Cathay Pacific, Japan Airlines and All Nippon Airways for the fast growing Pacific region. United agreed to co-ordinate the overall airline responses, and many of the airlines had resident representatives working with the design team, achieving performance more pertinent to their needs, rather than just falling short.

Boeing also had a need to reduce costs wherever possible and introduced 'concurrent engineering' and 'design/build' concepts into its organisation. This brought not only the design and manufacturing teams much closer together to understand each others problems, but also the suppliers and customers. This is expected to eliminate many expensive changes early in the programme.

Below:
Early studies of the 767-X looked at a fuselage stretch of the 767 with new wings and more powerful engines.

The Boeing 777 eventually evolved as a completely new aircraft taking advantage of all the latest technology.

Within a year Boeing was considering a new nine-abreast fuselage with a new wing; in effect a new aircraft, but aiming for the same type rating for pilots as the 757 and 767. British Airways was one of the interested customers and was urging for a go-ahead of the 767-X as it was now referred to, by the late summer of 1990 to allow them to make a decision on the TriStar replacement. In the latter part of 1989, Boeing was too heavily committed with other commercial aircraft programmes to be able to launch another new type.

Towards the end of 1989, the Japanese aerospace industry was indicating its interest in taking a substantial risk share in the proposed 767-X programme. Having already had the experience of the 767 business, Japan sought risk sharing partnerships, rather than just being a subcontractor, at an early stage. The common type rating was still a major consideration, to be achieved by fly-by-wire (FBW) to standardise the control inputs. Although the cockpit would be basically identical, liquid-crystal display flat panels would replace cathode ray tubes for the primary flight instrumentation.

At the end of 1989, the aircraft was beginning to take shape in its overall layout, with a new nine-abreast cabin capable of holding 350 two-class passengers, an all new wing with winglets

(which were later deleted) and a maximum take-off weight of 217,700kg. The 767 flight deck and tail were largely retained, but there was a new main six-wheel landing gear to take the additional weight. The shorter, but wider, fuselage overcame the problems of limited rotation at take-off with a long thin fuselage.

The Boeing board gave approval on 8 December 1989 for full marketing of the aircraft, which would be known as the Boeing 777 when a firm order was placed. Provisional performance included a range of 7,800-10,700km depending on configuration and seating would vary between 300-400 passengers, depending upon the layout. All three major engine manufacturers had power plant proposals for the new aircraft: Rolls-Royce with the 32,670-34,500kg-thrust Trent; Pratt & Whitney with the 33,600-36,350kg PW4000 development; and General Electric with the all new 36,300kg GE90.

In early 1990 it was reported that Japanese industry were keen for a 25% share in the 767-X $3.4 billion development costs, in return for a similar share in the production programme. However, with no agreement concluded by March, doubts were being voiced on the Japanese involvement in the 767-X, with Boeing looking further afield for partners, as well as continuing discussions with the Japanese. Agreement eventually came with a 21% Japanese investment in the programme in early 1991.

The 767-X began to evolve as a family of at least four versions, based on the 350-375-seat medium-range versions and including a

Left:
The wide cabin of the 777 gives the flexibility for a range of cabin interiors, especially with the seat rail-mounted stowages.

Right:
Using the latest technology of 3-D computer systems in the design of the 777, Boeing was able to reduce paperwork and avoid the construction of full-size mock-ups.

Far right:
The Boeing 777 two-crew flightdeck takes full advantage of the latest digital technology based upon operational experience with the 747-400.

stretched aircraft carrying up to 500 passengers for the Japanese market. Major dimensions would include a 60m wingspan, and a circular 620cm diameter fuselage. To take advantage of the latest flightdeck technology, the cockpit design was to be based on the 747-400, abandoning the common type rating with the 757/767. Initial maximum gross weight was targeted at 226,800kg and a range of 7,400-8,300km (4,000-4,500nm). The next development would have its maximum gross weight increased by 10%, a reduction of seating capacity to 290 and a range of about 11,400km (6,100nm).

The new advanced aerofoil wing should have an area of 416m^2 (4,480sq ft), giving a higher cruise Mach number and good approach speeds. All versions were expected to have the same basic engines rated at 69,000lb (307kN) thrust with the larger range versions at 75,000lb (333kN), and the power plants derated on the lighter models.

A further version would have at least an 8m fuselage stretch, about equivalent to the Boeing 747, with seats for up to 400 passengers and a range of 7,400km.

The fourth version of the 777 would be an ultra long-range aircraft capable of 13,500km (7,300nm) with 84,000lb (373kN) thrust engines and a maximum gross weight of around 272,000kg.

Pending the issue of a firm specification from Boeing, British Airways delayed its TriStar/DC-10 replacement decision; the competition being from the Airbus A300/A340 and the McDonnell Douglas MD-11. The BA requirement was for a 260-300 seater for London to the US West Coast, and more seats for short-haul routes such as London-Paris.

To reduce drawing paperwork drastically, much of the design work is being done on 3-D computers for both computer-aided design (CAD) and computer-aided manufacture (CAM). This allows accurate assessments of interfaces before components are built, avoiding expensive modifications at the systems integration stage. So confident are Boeing in the new technology that there are no plans to build full scale engineering mock-ups.

By late April 1990 the 767-X designation was also being referred to as the 'proposed 777' and two major markets were being identified as the transcontinental 'A' market and intercontinental 'B' market. More powerful engine options were being considered giving new performance. The 'A' market gross take-off weight had grown by 4,000kg to 231,750kg giving a base line range of 5,300 miles, and the 'B' market leaped nearly 11,000kg to 261,000kg giving a base line range of 7,600 miles. All three major engine manufacturers submitted larger thrust engines to cope with the increased power requirement.

In mid-1990, Boeing tried to tempt Cathay Pacific away from their A330-300 options by offering a new version of the 767-X, known as the 767-XS or the 'C' market 767-X. At the same time, Boeing revealed new overall details of the 767-X, including an optional wing fold, reducing span by 40ft (12.18m) to allow the aircraft to be compatible with DC-10 size gates at US hubs; and the new technology 747-400 lookalike flightdeck. Cathay's need was to carry up to 440 passengers on the 8,320km high-density Singapore

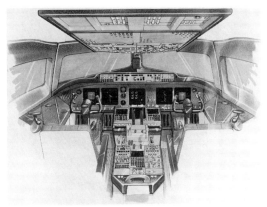

routes replacing Boeing 747-200s. The basic 767-X brought Melbourne, Dubai, Moscow and Anchorage within non-stop range of Hong Kong, but the extra endurance 767-XS could bring the key destinations of London, Rome, Frankfurt and Vancouver within reach.

New materials featured widely in the 767-X; the horizontal stabiliser, for example, being made primarily from composites. The whole section was designed for automatic fabrication. A major technological change was the introduction of a pitch-stability augmentation system, designed to improve aerodynamic performance throughout the full flight envelope, and to cope with the greater pitch changes associated with the longer fuselage and fuel transfer trim alterations. The system reduced drag, weight by 475kg and tail area by 19.5m^2.

On the flightdeck, a four display Electronic Flight Instrumentation System (EFIS) and two display Engine Indication and Crew Alerting System (EICAS) were featured on flat panel displays. Destination diversion information and an electronic checklist will be amongst the features in the system. Other cockpit features included satellite communications, VHF TV monitoring stations, dual ACARS data links, provision for microwave landing system (MLS), collision avoidance, global positioning systems and full provision for dual X-band weather radar.

Engine options still centred around the all new GE90 with thrust levels from 365kN to 423kN depending on fan size, the PW4076 ranging between 316kN to 400kN and the RR Trent 800 from 316kN to 400kN, the latter with a new core.

United Airlines, which had participated in the co-ordination of data from all the consultant airlines, was targeted as the possible lead customer, but had to postpone talks with the manufacturers in mid-1990 due to the refinancing of the airline. The planned launch of the 777 programme by Boeing, therefore, had to be delayed from the hoped for July time scale.

A major new innovation was announced by Boeing in July 1990 with their goal of the 777 operating under EROPS conditions from its initial service entry, rather than having to wait for the normal systems reliability proving period. To achieve this Boeing needed the authorities to adapt the regulations to allow immediate 180min EROPS clearance. The FAA was the lead authority with which Boeing was negotiating, and the benefits could also assist the EROPS operations of the competing MD-11 and A330. The key to agreement would centre largely around proven engine reliability which, on the face of it, could rule out new engines, such as the GE90, at least until it has had time to prove itself in service. Both Rolls-Royce and Pratt & Whitney would have to convince the authorities that their engines were derivatives. However, hopefully to overcome regulatory objections, Boeing planned to dedicate at least one extra aircraft to the development programme, specialising in EROPS validation. This would be backed up by extensive engineering simulations and a new systems integration facility. If Boeing did not achieve instant EROPS, they would at least expect to have an improvement on the two years of operations proving required.

Boeing formally launched the 777 programme on 29 October 1990, committing the company to achieve deliveries to United Airlines in mid-1995. United had placed the initial order on 15 October for the new aircraft, specifying 34 firm commitments and a further 34 options. The largest order in aviation history, worth $22 billion, also included up to 60 Boeing 747-400s. Pratt & Whitney won the engine order, worth about $4 billion with the PW4073 rated initially at 328.5kN (73,000lb) thrust. The United 777s, based on the 'A' market format, are to seat 363 passengers in dual-class configuration and will have a maximum take-off weight of 234,000kg and a range of up to 7,700km (4,200nm). The unique folding wing tip design was not specified in the order

even though United made the original request for operation from the existing DC-10 gates at Chicago O'Hare.

The circular fuselage section will have a 20ft 4in (6.2m) diameter. The round fuselage section, the first on a Boeing commercial jet transport, gave what the airlines wanted above and below the main floor. The above floor gave the maximum cabin area with a good maximum headroom and more storage volume per passenger than any other transport. The cabin also had a very high percentage of constant cross-section giving greater flexibility of layout without fuselage taper restrictions. The galleys and toilets are to be seat-rail mounted to allow a wide range of seating combinations to be used. The new circular fuselage section also allows the use of standard LD-3 containers in the underfloor cargo hold, a shortcoming with the 767, which could only use the specially designed LD-2 containers.

All Nippon Airways (ANA) were keen to take advantage of sharing the launch customer benefits, but their decision was delayed until at least the end of November to allow further evaluation of the competing Airbus A300/A340 and the MD-11. Following these evaluations, ANA then placed their order for 15 of the 'A'-market 777s at the end of November, with options on 10

more. Seating was for 400 in high density layout for domestic operations.

The Boeing 777 was treated as a separate division with its own executive vice president and about 4,000 people assigned to the programme at Renton in early 1991, growing to 10,000 people by mid-1992. By mid-1991 construction was planned to start on three major new buildings at Everett, the home of the 747 and 767. These buildings will consist of office accommodation for the programme teams, a large major sub-assembly facility and the third will be a vast new final assembly hall.

Boeing continued to press for EROPS approval improvements, submitting two sets of initial proposals, after working with the airlines, FAA, the engine and major system suppliers to define the criteria for early EROPS certification. The two sets of proposals covered aircraft type design approval, and the other for operations clearance for the 777 operators. Boeing had targeted a five-year development programme for the new aircraft, as compared with four years for the 767, which should give the additional time required to prove EROPS operations. This would be achieved on Boeing tests with each of the specified engines, and route proving with the launch customers, of which United would fly a

1,000 cycle programme. The current EROPS criteria called for individual airframe/engine combinations to demonstrate an in-flight shut down (IFSD) rate of no worse than 0.05 per 1000 flights, in order to fly 120min on the remaining engine from the nearest diversion airfield. Airlines which have amassed at least 12 months of EROPS experience at the 120min limit may apply for 180min clearance. However, to achieve this they must demonstrate an IFSD rate of 0.02 per 1,000 flights. This is roughly equivalent to one shutdown per aircraft every seven years at an average 9.3hr/day utilisation.

To make the 777 more acceptable to instant EROPS, Boeing was analysing all the reasons for turning back or diversion to alternative airports, excluding weather diversions. This would allow Boeing to incorporate design features to overcome the in-service experience largely achieved on the world-wide operations of the 767 fleet. First flight of the 777 is planned for June 1994 with certification and the first delivery to United in May 1995.

The launch customer for the 'B' market 777 was Euralair which ordered two aircraft in June 1991. These aircraft had the maximum gross take-off weight increased to 263,080kg and a range of 12,220km. The engine decision

remained to be made and deliveries were to be in 1997. At the Paris Show in the same month, Thai Airways became the fourth 777 customer with firm orders for six aircraft worth $900 million, and options on another six, subject to government approval. Once again, the engine decision was left open, the Thai order being for the 'A' market regional aircraft.

On 21 August 1991 British Airways placed their order for the Boeing 777, causing not only a major political storm in Europe with Airbus, but also with Rolls-Royce in their choice of the GE engines. British Airways placed a $3.6 billion order for 15 777s and options on another 15. At the same time, BA committed themselves to further 747-400s and British Aerospace ATPs. After taking bids from all the major engine manufacturers, BA agreed in principle to sell its profitable Welsh-based engine overhaul facility to GE, although a direct connection was denied. Deliveries of the 777s to BA will start in September 1995 with the first five in the 'A' market configuration. This short to medium-range model will be used on the US East Coast and Middle Eastern routes. The remaining firm orders and all the options will be the 'B' market long-range models for the airline's intercontinental routes. All the aircraft will have a three-class 313-passenger layout, with deliveries completed by 2002. The GE90 engine order has a potential value of $1.4 billion with certification due in November 1994 at 388.8kN (87,400lb) thrust. Not only were Rolls-Royce concerned at losing this order, but the effect it may have on other potential customers for the 777, who would have expected British Airways to have at least ordered British engines.

In early October 1991 Rolls-Royce received another setback to the launch of their Trent 870 Programme, when ANA selected Pratt & Whitney PW4073s to power their fleet of 777s. Rolls-Royce still hoped for the Thai order for the Trent engines, but the overall package still awaited formal approval.

In September 1991 Niki Lauda, of Lauda Air, announced an order for four Boeing 777s worth $560 million. The aircraft were to replace the airline's current fleet of 767s, with delivery of two aircraft in 1997 and the other two in 2000. This order was confirmed in October.

The sixth customer for the 777 was Japan Airlines with orders for the 10 aircraft and 10 options in November 1991. The firm orders were for the 'A' market domestic and regional use, while the options could include also some of the intercontinental 'B' market models. The engine choice was not made at this stage and deliveries were scheduled from late 1995 through to 1999. The cabin layout would be for 380 passengers in a two-class layout, and the folding wing tip option was declined.

Just prior to Christmas 1991, it was reported that Rolls-Royce had won an order worth £250 million for Trent engines to power Boeing 777s for Emirates, the Dubai-based airline. Emirates' intention was to order seven 777s with options on seven more. In their letter of intent Emirates

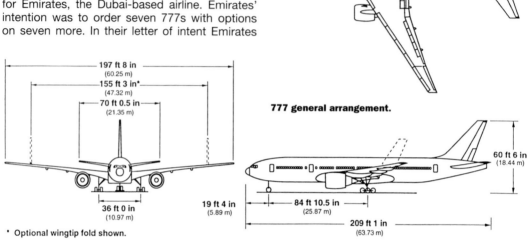

197 ft 8 in (60.25 m)
155 ft 3 in* (47.32 m)
70 ft 0.5 in (21.35 m)
36 ft 0 in (10.97 m)

777 general arrangement.

60 ft 6 in (18.44 m)
19 ft 4 in (5.89 m)
84 ft 10.5 in (25.87 m)
209 ft 1 in (63.73 m)

* Optional wingtip fold shown.

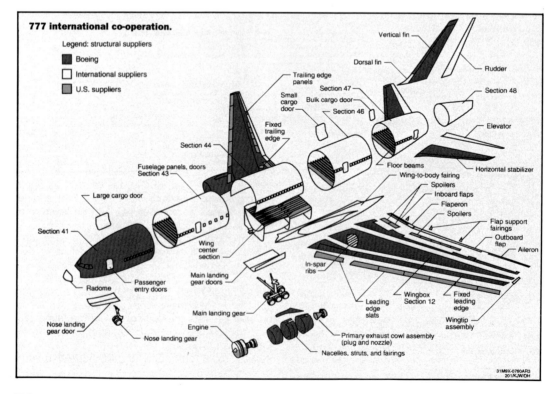

777 international co-operation.

Legend: structural suppliers

- ■ Boeing
- □ International suppliers
- ▨ U.S. suppliers

Vertical fin
Dorsal fin
Rudder
Trailing edge panels
Section 47
Section 48
Small cargo door
Bulk cargo door
Section 46
Fixed trailing edge
Elevator
Section 44
Floor beams
Horizontal stabilizer
Fuselage panels, doors Section 43
Wing-to-body fairing
Spoilers
Inboard flaps
Flaperon
Spoilers
Large cargo door
Flap support fairings
Section 41
Outboard flap
Aileron
Wing center section
In-spar ribs
Passenger entry doors
Main landing gear doors
Leading edge slats
Wingbox Section 12
Fixed leading edge
Radome
Main landing gear
Wingtip assembly
Nose landing gear door
Engine
Primary exhaust cowl assembly (plug and nozzle)
Nose landing gear
Nacelles, struts, and fairings

31M9X-0760AR3
201/KJW/DH

Left:
The larger Rolls-Royce Trent engine, as a development of the RB211 family, is specified by some of the customers for the early 777 models. Further growth versions will be used on later versions of the 777. *Rolls-Royce*

requested three 'A' models for 1996 delivery and the remainder with options, the 'B' model. The cabin width was of particular interest to the airline, the 10-abreast seating allowing a full load of 375 passengers on the less critical range operations. The Trent 877 engines are expected to develop 350kN (77,000lb) thrust on the improved 777A+ currently on offer. It is likely that these aircraft would be replaced by new ones when the 382kN Trent 844 engined 777B was delivered.

Lauda Air was expected to choose the GE90 engines for its 777s, and in February 1992 Thai Airways received government approval for their 777 order selecting the Rolls Royce Trent engine. The government approval increased the firm order to eight aircraft and brought all three engine manufacturers into the commercial programme.

At the time of writing, in February 1992, Boeing were revealing details of a proposed stretched version of the 777 under development for early service entry. The stretch being considered was 31ft (9.6m) of the fuselage particularly for the Asian market. The extension would be equally added around the wing centre section bringing overall length to around 73m. The current versions are the 777-200A and B models, externally identical at 63.7m long.

Development of the first aircraft was progressing ahead of programme with assembly of the early components in hand. First major assemblies were due to commence in April 1993, ready for a maiden flight in mid-1994.

In March 1990 Boeing donated the 747 prototype to the Seattle Museum of Flight. However, in February 1992, they leased it back as a flying test bed for the Pratt & Whitney and Rolls-Royce engines for the 777. The No 2 engine pylon attachment points and local wing structure were modified and strengthened. The first engine to be tested will be the PW4084 flying in June 1993. The RR Trent 884 is due to start its flight testing about one year later. The GE90 engine will be tested on another 747-100 on lease and operated from Mojave, California.

The Boeing 777 is therefore becoming established gradually in world markets, despite the depressed economics. Probably the most significant aircraft launched by Boeing since the 747, the 777 uses new technology where it pays for itself, the fly-by-wire controls being one of a number of firsts for Boeing. Unlike the launch of the 747, Boeing now have competition from McDonnell Douglas with the MD-11 and from Europe in the form of the Airbus A330/A340 family of airliners.

12. Recent Developments

Boeing 757

Sales of the 757-200 series have continued over the last seven years, earning a good income and surviving the various world and regional economic crises. Regrettably, there have also been a modest number of losses from which lessons have been learned, even though there was no inherent fault with the aircraft.

In a surprise move in early 1992, UPS selected Rolls-Royce to power its second batch of 757 freighters, even though the initial batch of 20 aircraft were Pratt & Whitney-powered. Options on Rolls-Royce engines for a further 41 757s had also been taken. Also at the end of 1991 Shanghai Airlines ordered five PW2000-powered 757s to add to the three already in operation. The Dutch charter carrier Transavia introduced its first two 757s in April and May 1992. The world recession caused major difficulties even for the normally healthy major US airlines, Delta Air Lines being an example when it announced major fleet reductions in April 1992. Amongst the aircraft on firm order were 16 757s with options on 40 aircraft. On the more positive side, the Colombian carrier Avianca took delivery of the first of two 757s in August.

In July 1992 the Pratt & Whitney PW2000-powered 757 achieved 180min EROPS from the FAA, and was demonstrated by a 6hr inaugural flight by American Trans Air from Tucson, Arizona to Honolulu in Hawaii.

China had become a major Boeing customer with its developing air transport industry and in August 1992 a 757-200 for Xiamen Airlines became the 100th delivery to China, with two more on order. By mid-year Boeing had 56 outstanding Chinese orders to fulfil, of which about half were 757s. However, with only around 15 new orders taken during 1992 overall, Boeing was planning on cutting the production rate of the 757 from 8.5 per month to seven by June

Below:
Airtours operates a fleet of seven 757s on holiday charter flights from a number of UK airports. G-RJGR was the eighth aircraft off the line and originally delivered to Eastern Airlines. This early production aircraft was seen at London Gatwick in July 1998. *Author*

1993, falling to five by the following November. In December United announced reductions in deliveries of a number of Boeing airliners, but the 757 survived unscathed. Boeing had already delivered 71 757s out of the total of 90 on order with the expectation of firming up a further four 757 options. On a more positive note, ILFC announced major orders for 19 757s with options on five, plus 10 767s with five options and six 777s with two options.

In January 1993 Britannia Airways ordered seven 757-200ERs to replace the last of its 737s, deliveries of the new aircraft starting in May 1994. This order was in addition to the seven 757s already on order, with first deliveries imminent. In March Air Seychelles doubled its Boeing fleet when a Rolls-Royce-powered 757-200ER was delivered to be used on routes to Johannesburg and Singapore. In May Continental Airlines placed an order for 92 Boeing airliners with 98 options, including 50 757s, 30 767s and 10 777s. In the same month Ambassador Airways began services from Newcastle with two 757s to Greek and Cyprus resorts, and in July China Southern announced plans to lease a further four 757s. In November UPS ordered 10 more Rolls-Royce-powered 757 freighters to add to the 55 already ordered or delivered. At the end of the year ILFC topped up its order book with five 757-200s, bringing the total sales for the year to 40 757s.

In January 1994, Northwest Airlines announced major cancellations of airliner orders as a result of the struggle for survival over the previous year. Although no 757s were cancelled, 40 deliveries were deferred for an average of 3.5 years, and options on a further 40 757s were cancelled. However, in early 1995 Northwest decided to take 15 757s earlier than scheduled, with deliveries in 1995 and 1996, but the next 25 were deferred until 2003-5. The airline already had 33 757-200s in operation.

With the change of regime in the former USSR, a number of private airlines were challenging the state-owned Aeroflot. The most successful of these airlines is Transaero which became the first Russian airline to operate the 757 when the first of two leased examples was delivered in April 1994. A further two 757s were added in 1995 for services to Berlin and Frankfurt. In June Baikal Airlines put a single Rolls-Royce-powered 757 leased from ILFC into service from Irkutsk to Moscow. Also in June, Air China was reported to be negotiating for up to 15 757s, amongst other Boeing airliners, although in July an 18-month moratorium on the order of new airliners was announced while the infrastructure was put in order, due to the high number of accidents. During the first half of

1994 one 757 had been delivered to each of China Southern and China Southwest, with a further 11 757s on order for China Southwest. In September 1994 American Trans Air (ATA) signed a letter of intent with ILFC for two 757-200s to add to the six already operated by the airline, and signed a letter of intent with Boeing for a further six 757-200s.

In April 1995 United ordered five 757s, as well as two 747-400s for delivery by June 1996, the fleet already containing 88 757s. On 28 September Lineas Aereas Privadas Argentinas (LAPA) took delivery of its first 757 with plans to consider a further aircraft six months later. In October 1995 two 767-300ERs and one 757 were ordered by Uzbekistan Airways, and the National Civil Aviation Authority of Turkmenistan ordered two 757s to add to the one already in operation.

The end of 1995 into 1996 was a bad year for 757 accidents. However, even though they were partly due to crew error, lessons were learned by studying the effects of crew actions to avoid repetition.

On 20 December 1995 American Airlines 757-200 N651AA flying from Miami to Cali in Colombia crashed into mountains at night killing all but four of the people on board. The aircraft was on its descent into Cali when it hit a 12,000ft (3,660m) mountain at a height of about 9,000ft near the town of Buga around 18km (10nm) east of the normal let-down track. All the navigation beacons were working, there was no immediate reason for the aircraft to be so far off track, while the cockpit voice recorder (CVR) and the flight data recorder (FDR) gave no indication of any technical problems. The ground proximity warning system alerted the crew too late to take avoiding action. It was soon established from the readout of the CVR that the crew failed to carry out pre-descent approach briefing or checks before entering the steep-sided valley and flew into the side of the mountain while becoming established on the approach.

On 6 February 1996 Turkish charter airline Birgenair 757-200 TC-GEN had departed the Dominican Republic at night and was climbing through 7,000ft (2,000m) when the crew called Approach Control to advise that a return was being made to the airport. Following the words 'stand by', there were no more messages and the aircraft fell into the sea some 20km (11nm) north of Puerto Plata, killing all 176 passengers and 13 crew. The aircraft was en route to Berlin and Frankfurt via Gander and the weather at the time was light rain. The FDR and CVR were recovered from the seabed by the US Navy by the end of the month, a faulty captain's airspeed indicator emerging as a possible factor in the accident. The FDR showed an indicated air-speed (IAS) of 335kt (620km/h) when the stall warning stick shaker activated at 7,300ft (2,200m), but the normal stalling speed is about 130kt IAS. The stick shaker operated for 83sec before the aircraft crashed, the pilots failing to recover from the stall. From analysis of the CVR, the crew were aware that the captain's ASI was not working correctly, and elected to use the first officer's. The crew failed to consult the checklists or manuals, nor did they compare the main ASIs with the standby unit. The aircraft had been parked at Puerto Plata since 23 January and the appropriate pitot head cov-ers had not been used. Soon after take-off, the captain engaged the autopilot in the climb which is slaved to the air-data computer, which senses airspeed from the captain's ASI. As the height increased the captain's ASI began to read higher than the correct speed, and as a result the autopilot/autothrottle increased pitch up and reduced power to lower the apparent airspeed. Due to crew confusion the aircraft stalled and was out of control for 1min 4sec before hitting the sea.

The third 757 to be lost was N52AW operat-ed by Aero Peru which crashed into the Pacific Ocean on 2 October 1996 killing all 70 people on board. The aircraft was flying from Lima in Peru to Santiago in Chile, and shortly after take-off the crew requested a return to Lima with 'mechanical problems'. After a 30min conversa-tion between the crew and ATC, radar contact was lost, and the aircraft crashed into the sea off Pasamayo, some 40nm (75km) north of Lima, at night and in fog. The captain had reported losing the basic instruments for height and speed, and despite reducing power, the air-craft still appeared to be accelerating. Following the investigation, it was found that during main-tenance the static vents had been taped over

for protection, but the tape had not been removed prior to flight causing the captain to lose control.

In February 1996, TWA announced that it would be replacing 14 Lockheed TriStars and some 727s with a fleet of 20 Pratt & Whitney-powered 757s, 10 of which were purchased direct from Boeing, and the balance leased from ILFC. Options were taken on a further 20 air-craft, the ordered 757s being delivered at the rate of three in 1996, 12 in 1997 to replace the TriStars on domestic operations, plus two in 1998 and three in 1999 to replace 727s. In effect TWA was replacing a three-engined, three-crew aircraft with a more economic two-engined, two-crew aircraft. The first of the new 757s entered service on 1 August 1996 between St Louis and Orange County in California.

By March 1996, Boeing had progressed well on the definition of the 757-300, with German charter operator Condor, with a fleet of 18 757-200s favoured as the possible launch. The 757-300X is a simple stretch of the earlier version with two plugs inserted fore and aft of the wing-box to increase the overall capacity by some 20% from around 198 to 235 passengers, while maintaining the range close to the existing 5,550km (3,000nm). It was expected that seat costs would fall by around 10%, making the air-craft attractive to many of the existing European charter operators and engine power would be increased modestly using derivatives of existing

Rolls-Royce RB211-535E4s and Pratt &Whitney PW2043s.

In April 1996 Finnair selected four 757s for its charter operations, the first Boeing airliners to be acquired by the airline. The 219-seat 757s were for direct routes to the Canary Islands, Middle East and India, with the possibility later of transatlantic operations. The lease was confirmed with ILFC in July with the first delivery in September 1997 and service entry on 24 October. A new Manchester-based airline, Flying Colours, was launched in April 1996 with an order for four new RB211-535E4-powered 757s under lease in time for operations to commence in the 1997 holiday season, three of the aircraft to be based at Manchester and the other at Gatwick. The first aircraft was delivered on 26 February with services beginning on 6 March. In June 1998 Flying Colours was taken over by Sunworld which operated Airworld, but the Flying Colours identity and most of the senior management were retained. As part of an overall order for Boeing airliners in May 1996, United included five Pratt & Whitney-powered 757s.

The stretched 757-300 was launched at the Farnborough airshow in September 1996 with an order for 12 aircraft and 12 options from Condor, subject to the approval of the airline board, with deliveries to commence in 1999. The 7.1m stretch would allow up to 289 passengers to be carried, although Condor planned for a total of 252 seats. The underfloor cargo capacity was also increased by 40%, and the range increased to 3,500nm (6,430km). Other orders announced by Boeing at the same time included five 757-200s for ILFC and three for BA, the latter being confirmed in March 1997. Delta also ordered four more PW2037-powered 757-200s from ILFC in mid-September to replace 737s on the low-fare Delta Express operations. By the end of the month of September, total deliveries of the 757 had reached 699 aircraft, with a backlog of 102 aircraft, taking total sales to 801 aircraft.

In January 1997 Mexicana introduced its first two P&W Boeing 757-200s on lease from ILFC with plans to later add a third aircraft. In March, Continental Airlines added 16 firm orders for RB211-powered 757s, increasing the airline's fleet to 41 aircraft. American Airlines restructured its orders with Boeing in May 1997 with 12 757s being delivered at the rate of one per month, starting in June 1998, and purchase rights maintained on a further 38 aircraft. Icelandair added to its 757 fleet in June 1997 by placing an order for a pair of Rolls-Royce-powered 757-200s, and became the second customer for the stretched version by ordering two 757-300s. Options on a further eight 757s were taken, the first delivery being of a 757-200 in January 1998.

In June 1997 the original Boeing 757 prototype was converted as a flying test-bed for the F-22 Raptor fighter programme, and delivered after conversion to Boeing Field at Seattle later the same month. The aircraft nose had a typical 2.7m-long F-22 section forward of the cockpit bulkhead fitted to house the APG-77 radar and a 9m-span test wing was fitted on the crown of the fuselage in August 1998. The fuselage was fitted out with a 30-seat-plus laboratory containing the full range of electronic warfare, communications, navigation and identification sensors to allow full avionics testing to commence in August 1998. The aircraft had originally been an avionics test laboratory, and was initially modified to support the YF-22 avionics integration during the Advanced Tactical Fighter competition.

On the military side four 757s were sold to the USAF. They were designated C-32As, the first one making the maiden flight from Renton on 11 February 1998. Unlike previous military transports for the USAF, the C-32As were treated as standard commercial aircraft. The 2hr first flight was completed with a landing at Boeing Field where development testing continued. The 45-passenger aircraft were ordered to replace the ageing C/VC-137s with the 89th Airlift Wing at Andrews AFB in Maryland for government communications.

In November 1997, Taiwan's Far Eastern Air Transport (FEAT) signed a letter of intent for five 757-200s for delivery in 1999, and options on another five aircraft. Although it did not add to the overall sales total, Greenlandair took delivery of its first jet airliner, an ex-Rolls-Royce-powered Airtours International example, which entered service between Greenland and Copenhagen on 12 May.

Major assembly of sub-components for the first 757-300 began at Renton in November 1997 with manufacturing of the front left wing spar commencing in September. It was the first time that the automated spar assembly tool (ASAT) had been used for the 757, and it is capable of automatic drilling and installation of more than 2,600 fasteners into the wing, reducing time and cost, as well as improving quality. The front and rear fuselage sections were joined

to the centre-section in March 1998 making it the longest single-aisle twinjet to be built, with a length of 54.4m. The first aircraft was rolled out at Renton on 31 May with three 757-300s expected to participate in the flight development programme, taking some 725hr, with certification scheduled for December 1998 and first delivery the following month. At the time of roll-out, Condor added one more -300 to its order, while discussions were going on with a number of domestic US operators. The maiden flight was scheduled for 1 July, but the overall production problems at Renton caused a delay until 2 August when the first aircraft lifted off the Renton runway for a 2½hr maiden flight. Under the command of chief project and test pilot Leon Robert assisted by senior project pilot Jerry Whites, a maximum altitude of 16,000ft and maximum speed of 250kt were reached, as well as some general handling being done.

Below:
The first major development of the Boeing 757 is the stretched -300 which is 23ft 7in longer than the earlier aircraft. Both types are produced on the same line at the Renton facility to the east of Seattle. The stretched fuselage gives accommodation for 20% more passengers, and the cargo volume is increased by nearly 50%. *Boeing*

Above right:
The first Boeing 757-300 made its maiden flight from Renton on 2 August 1998 in the hands of Leon Robert and Jerry Whites, landing after 2½hr at Boeing Field at Seattle. Initial customers for this version are Condor, Icelandair and Arkia. *Boeing*

Boeing 767

The AWACS version of the 767 was revealed for the first time in early 1992 since not only was the 707 airframe becoming somewhat out of date, but a substantial order would be required to make it economical to return it to production. The best prospect for the new version of the 767 was the Japanese government which had a need for four aircraft, with Australia as another prospect and there were also requirements by Italy, South Korea, Turkey and Saudi Arabia. The most obvious external change to the airframe was the mounting of the distinctive rotating radome above the rear portion of the fuselage to give all-round coverage. With many of the cabin windows deleted, the main cabin is reconfigured with the installation of the specialist communications and data processing equipment to allow the crew at up to nine mission control stations to detect numbers of hostile aircraft, and guide the defending aircraft and missiles to neutralise the threat.

Finally the long-awaited launch order from Japan for the E-767, as the project had become known, was announced in November 1993 for an initial two aircraft, powered by GE CF6-80C2. The aircraft, which were based on the 767-200ER, were built on the regular production line at Everett and then flown to the Boeing facility at Wichita in Kansas in October 1994 for the strengthening of the airframe structure in the main cabin to accept the radome, and the installation of the large electrical power generation and distribution system.

The first airframe then returned to Everett where it was painted and the radome fitted ready for the official maiden flight on 9 August 1996. This aircraft was used for aerodynamic testing for an initial seven months before the fitting and integration of the prime mission equipment. By this time the order had been increased to four aircraft with deliveries of the first pair in March 1998, to be followed by the other two in January 1999. The installation and integration of the mission-system equipment commenced at Seattle in May 1997 and on 11 March 1998 handover of the first two E-767s, the next pair were parked alongside at Boeing Field as they were prepared for later delivery. Following the delivery of the first two E-767s to Japan, the next major prospect was seen as South Korea, with an initial requirement for four aircraft.

In addition to the E-767, Boeing has also proposed further military versions of the 767 as replacements for the progressively ageing KC-135 fleet with the USAF, in particular in the tanker/transport role, but as yet no firm orders have been placed.

The freighter version of the 767 based on the -300ER airframe was launched by UPS with an order for 30 aircraft in January 1993, to allow the operator to expand its domestic and international services. In addition to structural strengthening of the main undercarriage and wing structure, the 767 freighter was fitted with an upward-opening cargo door in the forward cabin on the port side, and all cabin windows were deleted. UPS selected the GE CF6-80C2 with harmful emissions reduced by some 40%. The UPS specification called for what Boeing considered to be an interim freighter, as to keep costs to a minimum there was no main deck powered cargo handling system, only basic galley and toilet systems were fitted, and because no live cargo or perishable loads were carried by UPS, fire suppression systems were not installed. However, the launch customer for the full-specification freighter was Asiana of South Korea with an initial requirement for two aircraft.

The UPS programme was very tight with assembly of the first aircraft commencing at Everett in January 1995 ready for roll-out of the first aircraft in May. The maiden flight followed at

the end of June, commencing the certification programme involving three aircraft on flight and ground tests, which was completed in time for the first aircraft to be handed over on 12 October, to be followed by four more aircraft by mid-November, in time for the Christmas rush. Asiana took delivery of the first of two full-specification freighters in August 1996. In April 1998, UPS announced a need for further freighter aircraft to replace its ageing DC-8s. Boeing proposed a special freighter conversion of the 767-200 using existing airframes. The competition came from used Airbus A300B4s and TriStars, many of which were readily available for reasonable prices.

Airborne Express acquired 12 ex-All Nippon 767-200s for conversion to freighter configuration by Timco in early 1996, the first three of which entered the conversion programme in early 1998, the first being completed by May with certification and service entry expected by July.

Since 1992, Boeing had been studying long-range and higher capacity versions of the 767. Initial studies concentrated on extending the range of the 767-300ER with increased fuel capacity and modifications to the wing structure including increasing the chord and adding winglets. However, by early 1997 the programme had changed to an increased capacity aircraft known as the 767-400ERX with formal approval from the Boeing board to offer the aircraft to airline customers on 6 January.

In a controversial exclusive fleet renewal deal signed between Boeing and Delta Air Lines in March 1997 covering the potential purchase of up to 644 aircraft, the new 767-400 was included, launching the programme. The initial contract for the stretched 767-400 was for 21 firm orders with options on 24, and further commitments to another 25 aircraft. First deliveries of the -400s on firm order were scheduled in 2000

Above:
Airborne Express bought 10 surplus All Nippon 767-200s for conversion to freighter configuration with a cargo door in the forward cabin. The aircraft were delivered painted in the operator's colours before conversion to the new configuration. *Airborne Express*

Below right:
Britannia Airways, based at London Luton Airport, has been a major operator of Boeing products for a number of years, starting with the 737-200s. Britannia now operates a fleet of Boeing 767-200s and -300s as well as a number of 757-200s. These aircraft are used from a number of UK airports on holiday charter flights to destinations as far away as Australia, South Africa and North America. 767-204ER G-BPFV is now with Air Europa in Spain, but the airline still operates seven 767-200ERs, together with at least eight 767-304s, some of which operate with the newly formed German subsidiary. *Britannia Airways*

to replace the last of the TriStars with the airline. Also included in this order were a further 10 767-300ERs with options on a further 10 and commitments to 19, five firm 757s with options on 20 and commitments for a further 90 and 10 options on Trent-powered 777-200s. The remainder of the order was made up of the new-generation 737s. Three months later in June, Continental Airlines also signed a sole supplier deal with Boeing which included 30 767-400ERs for deliveries commencing in mid-2000. Included in the deal were five 777-200s with undisclosed options on both types. A further five 767-400s have been ordered by ILFC for undisclosed operators.

With the 767-400 firmly committed to enter service, detailed design engineering commenced for the aircraft to join the existing 767 models on the line at Everett. Advantage was taken of experience gained with the 777 and new-generation 737s to bring the aircraft systems up to date in the most cost-effective manner, and also to benefit from the lessons learned in production. The new flightdeck features six flat-panel liquid crystal displays using wherever possible 777 components. The digital displays are programmable to represent either the 'round dial' or the primary flight display (PFD) format allowing pilot ratings to be consistent across the Boeing airliner fleet, whether equipped with older, or new-generation aircraft. The cabin will feature a new-look design based on the 777, and in September 1997 Boeing began to investigate range increases as a result of the requirement from potential customers.

Meanwhile, sales of the existing 767s had continued from 1992, mainly as a top-up of the existing large fleets, or with some of the smaller airlines taking modest start-up orders. Examples of some of these fleet renewals included two 767-200ERs for Mozambique, two 767-300ERs for EVA Air, one 767-300ER for Malev delivered in May 1992 with two 767-200ERs delivered the following year, while American Airlines and ANA continued to increase their fleets. In September 1992 American already operated eight 767-200s, 22 767-200ERs and 25 767-300ERs with a further 16 -300ERs on order. Its fleet also included 49 757s. All Nippon ordered two more 767-300s in October 1993, bringing its total commitment to the twinjet to 63 aircraft, making it the largest customer outside the USA. By the end of 1993 United planned to be operating 19 767-200s and 23 767-300ERs as well as 88 757-200s.

Despite the recession, modest orders continued to be achieved including two 767-300ERs for Leisure Airways, a 767-300ER for Air Pacific to add to the 767-200ER already in service, and in early 1994 Aeroflot ordered four 767-300ERs, all these aircraft being operated under leases. Kazakhstan Airlines ordered four PW4056-powered 767-300ERs in early 1994, and KLM replaced its Airbus A310 fleet with seven leased 767-300ERs with three more added in mid-

1995. Britannia Airways, already an established Boeing customer, ordered at the end of 1994 four 767-300ERs with options on four more to add to its fleet of nine 767-200s and 19 757s. Rolls-Royce gained its second order for engines to power the 767 when China Yunnan selected three 767-300ERs in early 1995, replacing an earlier order for 757s.

With Air France experiencing economic difficulties, its order for seven 767s, as well as other Boeing types, was reduced to three aircraft in mid-1995. Alitalia leased three 767-300ERs in August 1995 to add to the two already leased in early 1995, the aircraft being operated by Monarch. Lauda Air added a fifth 767-300ER in August 1995 and LanChile took over Ladeco, bringing the combined fleet to five 767s and two 757s as well as other types, ordering three more -300ERs in mid-1997. Air Seychelles added a 767-300 to the 767-200ER in late 1996 to replace the 757 to increase passenger and cargo capacity. Three ex-Continental 767-300ERs were leased to Vietnam Airlines in early 1996 to replace wet-leased aircraft already in operation. Transaero, one of the independent Russian airlines, issued a tender in March 1996 for the supply of three 767s to add to the five 757s and other aircraft already being operated by the airline. By September 1996 total sales for the 767 had reached 690 aircraft with 605 delivered.

Also suffering from economic problems, Gulf Air disposed of six 767-300ERs to Delta Air Lines in March 1997, returning three of its stored TriStars to service. On a more positive note, BA ordered three additional 767-300ERs in mid-1997 for delivery in April and May 1998. Not having ordered any 767s for some time, United added eight more PW4000-powered 767-300ERs in mid-1997 with deliveries commencing in May 1998. The Belgian low-fare scheduled airline, Sobelair, which commenced

operation in early 1997, added a pair of 767-300ERs in early 1998. Asiana gained government approval in August to order an initial two passenger 767-300s, with a further two ordered in early 1998 as part of an overall fleet growth programme with Boeing and Airbus airliners.

With many of the airliners in service being leased, it was logical for the lease companies to place substantial orders, and ILFC included seven 767-300ERs, five of the new 767-400ERs and six 757-200ERs in its overall requirement for 126 new aircraft from Boeing and Airbus in September 1997. The Asian economic crisis which started in early 1998 put a number of airline orders in doubt, causing the manufacturers to review their production programmes.

In other regions modest sales continued to be made with Air Madagascar replacing its 747-200 with an interim-lease 767-300ER from April 1998 until a new aircraft could be delivered a year later. Similarly, Air Namibia replaced its 747SP with a 767-300ER on 1 April 1998 for services to Frankfurt and London. Air Europa took delivery of an ex-Asiana 767-300ER to operate on behalf of Iberia on services from Madrid to Chicago from March 1998, and the Russian independent Transaero put its first 767-300ER into service on the Moscow to Tel Aviv route in mid-1998.

The Boeing 767 therefore continues to attract a steady stream of orders, mostly from the lease companies, and further sales are assured with the developments, particularly the stretched -400ER, which will take production well into the next century and probably reach over 1,000 aircraft.

Boeing 777

Since the previous revision of this book, when the 777 was first dealt with, the aircraft has been developed, flight tested and entered service, with the new stretched 777-300 just beginning operations in mid-1998.

A major feature of the 777 programme was that Boeing changed its way of working, treating the customer as partner. This was not just the airline customer, but the suppliers, subcontractors and the Boeing workers as well, one of the actions being to form design/build teams to ensure that what the engineers designed could be produced by the most economic and practical methods. The early airline customers were involved in the design and specification of the aircraft, with access to Boeing's previously confidential information, and influenced aspects of aircraft operation, accessibility for servicing and maintenance and layout of the cabin. In fact, the 777 was designed around the cabin with what were known as 'flex-zones' to allow wide variations in the positioning of galleys and toilets depending upon passenger demand.

Even at the early stages of design, Boeing was looking at the overall development prospects of the new aircraft, the stretched version with accommodation for 60 more passengers being confirmed in mid-1992 for service entry in mid-1998. Cathay had already placed an order for 11 777s with 11 options, and was likely to be the launch customer for the stretched version.

Also by mid-1992, two years before the planned first flight date, the production of parts had commenced by over 40 major suppliers, subcontractors and risk-sharing partners from as far away as Australia, Japan, which were responsible for all the fuselage aft of the Boeing-built section 41, and Europe, making it an international programme. Another innovation was the systems integration laboratory (SIL), equivalent to a 777 without its skin, as part of an overall integrated aircraft-systems laboratory built at Seattle. The Dassault/IBM CATIA computer-aided engineering allowed three-dimensional checking of parts' interfaces, avoiding the need for an engineering mock-up for the first time, the accuracy being proven on a sample nose section. Where appropriate, new materials were introduced including a hardened aluminium alloy and an increased use of composites, particularly in major structural and load-bearing areas such as the fin, rudder, tailplane and elevators. The flightdeck was configured with liquid crystal full-colour flat-panel displays and equipped with an aircraft integrated management system (AIMS) and an integrated air-data/inertial reference system. A maintenance access terminal for AIMS is located on the flightdeck for quick access by engineering personnel for fault analysis. The 777 is also Boeing's first fly-by-wire airliner, but a conventional control column was retained, rather than change to the sidestick type of control used by Airbus.

By the end of 1992, Boeing was offering a heavier, longer range version to follow quickly after the initial A-market version. Fabrication of the first aircraft commenced in early 1993 with the nosewheel well in the forward lower fuselage, major fuselage sections were completed by August, and final assembly commenced in December. The roll-out of the first 777 was from the specially extended wide body plant at Everett on 9 April 1994, following which attention was given to ensuring the correct functioning of the aircraft systems with particular reference to the flight control software, the engine integration and the AIMS software, backed up

Above:
A new double-bay production hall was added to the factory facility at Everett for the building of the Boeing 777s. Following detail manufacture at the far end of the building, the airframe is assembled in the jig in the background, and then moved forward for the fitting of the engines and overall equipping, before being towed across the road to the paint shop. Following this the aircraft is prepared for flight on the flight line, when all the systems are checked. *Author*

Below:
United Airlines placed the launch order for the Boeing 777 in October 1990 with 32 firm orders and 32 options powered by P&W PW4000 engines. The first 16 aircraft were to the early standard, but the 777-222ERs followed on, replacing the earlier aircraft on the transatlantic operations. United 777-222ER N782UA was delivered to United on 7 March 1997 and is seen on approach to London Heathrow in May 1998. *Author*

by intense efforts in the integrated aircraft systems laboratory.

The Boeing 777 made its maiden flight of 3hr 48min from Everett on 12 June 1994, commanded by John Cashman assisted by Ken Higgins, director of flight test, the fly-by-wire flight control system working as expected. Following three more flights from Everett, the 777 began the full flight development programme of some 4,800 test flights from Boeing Field just south of Seattle. As well as planning to have an aircraft with full extended range operations (EROPS) approval on delivery to the airlines, it was also the goal of Boeing to have the aircraft service-ready, in other words achieving a reliability rate of over 98% on service entry, instead of three to four years into regular operations.

All three major engine manufacturers were offering engines for the 777 programme, probably the last time this will happen, since the cost of development of the airframe/engine combination makes it almost impossible for all three to obtain an economic return on the investment, particularly with the continuing demands by the airlines and Boeing for further improvements in performance, reliability and economy. While the Rolls-Royce Trent and the Pratt & Whitney PW4000 series were derivative engines, the General Electric GE90 was an all-new design, with greater potential for development than the other two engines, but at higher cost. The Rolls-Royce Trent 884 powerplant for the 777 made its first run in the Derby test cell on 8 October,

exceeding 84,000lb (375kN) thrust during the initial test. The first of the engines to fly was the Pratt &Whitney PW4084, when it flew on the Boeing 747 test-bed on 10 November 1993. This was followed by the GE90 on 6 December, and P&W became the first to achieve approval, when the FAA certification was achieved in May 1994. Although modest growth of the GE90 was agreed, GE eventually pulled out of major development investment, leaving the airlines which had specified the engine with the situation of having to change engine suppliers for later versions of the 777. Meanwhile Pratt & Whitney developed the 90,000lb thrust PW4090 to power the -200IGW with Korean and United, and Rolls-Royce was developing the Trent 800 to power the stretched -300.

By mid-1995 Boeing was looking at the market potential for a shorter ultra-long-range version of the 777 capable of carrying up to 250 passengers on the long thin routes of up to 9,000nm, but to date no progress has been made on this version, the airlines preferring the stretched 777-300ER, with Cathay being particularly keen, and Rolls-Royce prepared to provide the power. The 777-300 was formally launched at the Paris Air Show in June 1995 with orders for a total of 27 aircraft from ANA which ordered 10 with five options, Cathay which converted seven of its earlier order plus 11 options, Korean which ordered four new versions and Thai which ordered six new 777-300s. The new aircraft was designed to seat up to 550 passengers in single-class layout in a 10m longer fuselage, although between 368 and 394 passengers in a three-class layout was expected to be more the norm. The B-market aircraft, known as the -200IGW, entered assembly on 20 February 1996 for delivery to BA in early 1997, first flying on 7 October 1996 powered by the GE90 engines, and the 777-300 began major assembly in late March 1997. The first Trent-powered -200IGW destined for

Below:
British Airways was one of the few airlines to specify the GE90 engines when it placed its order for 20 Boeing 777s in August 1991, with options on a further 15 aircraft. The first five aircraft were produced to the initial standard, but the next 15 were 777-200ERs. Boeing 777-200ER G-VIIL, one of those painted in the new BA colours, is seen at London Gatwick in April 1998. *Nick Granger*

Emirates flew from Everett on 21 November 1996.

A major part of the flight development programme was the attempt to achieve EROPS on delivery of the 777 to the airlines, instead of waiting for two or three years while the systems were proved in service. This added a year to the flight test programme with three dedicated test aircraft powered by each of the three engines on offer. ETOPS had been the original concept, meaning extended-range twinjet operations over oceans up to 180min flying time from a suitable diversionary airfield, but it was felt unreasonable to penalise just the twinjets, when the same levels of reliability should be achieved with all modern jet airliners, resulting in EROPS as the standard to work to. The US FAA required some demanding conditions to achieve EROPS from day one, including 1,000 flight cycles achieved with each engine type on typical airline operation. One of the engines fitted for the demonstration should already have been through a 2,000 to 3,000-cycle ground test beforehand, and must operate for at least 500 cycles on the aircraft without significant failure, to qualify for 180min EROPS. The EROPS capability was not just dependent on the engines, but also the associated equipment including back-up power from the APU, and when certificated as an engine/airframe combination by the FAA, the airworthiness authority of the country in which the customer airline was based had also to approve the operating and maintenance standards of the airline before giving approval for EROPS. In addition, it may not be approved for the full 180min immediately. The European airworthiness authorities preferred a more conservative approach, considering 120min EROPS sufficient for a start into service, especially as such a limitation would be adequate for all the commercial routes across the Atlantic, whereas the 180min rule would be required for the longer Pacific routes. The British CAA was prepared to allow BA a 138min approval for the North Atlantic providing the demanding conditions were met. After a delay of about two months, Boeing was able to start EROPS testing of the P&W-powered 777 on 29 December 1994 using the fourth 777 which had made its first flight on 28 October. Out of the total of 1,000 representative flights, nearly 100 were operated by United air and ground crews under the supervision of Boeing.

The second P&W-powered 777, and the first for United, joined the flight development programme on 15 July 1994, and the fifth P&W-powered 777 was used to validate the EROPS certification testing. Early testing with the first 777 was at Edwards Air Force Base in California with further more demanding tests in October, including the rejected take-off, and the third aircraft joined the test programme on 2 August. The first GE90-powered 777 for BA entered the flight test programme on 2 February 1995 and the Trent 890 flew for the first time in the Boeing 747 test bed on 29 March. Certification was finally achieved from both the FAA and the European JAA on 19 April 1995 of the P&W-powered 777 ready for delivery to United on 15 May, while 180min EROPS testing continued on target for award on 30 May, a week before service entry. The overall flight test programme for the 777-200 alone was estimated to have taken 6,700 flight hours over more than 4,800 cycles, using nine aircraft, of which three were allocated exclusively to EROPS certification. The first Trent-powered 777 made its first flight on 26 May in the colours of Cathay Pacific, its first aircraft being delivered in May 1996. The Boeing 777 entered service with United on 7 June between London and Chicago service-ready, as aimed for by Boeing and United from the start of the programme. The EROPS testing of the GE90-powered 777 for BA was seriously delayed by problems with the engine, the original approval being required in September 1995, but the flight test programme of 1,000 cycles did not start until April 1996, a month after the start of the Trent tests, which received FAA approval in early April 1997 ready for Emirates to take delivery of its first -200IGW in June. The first GE-powered 777 for BA arrived at Heathrow on 12 November 1995 following certification on 3 November, but was not cleared for EROPS, the initial services being to Paris and the Middle East to build up experience with the type and increase capacity to Dubai and Muscat. Transatlantic 777 flights were initiated by BA on 27 October 1996 following initial approval for EROPS.

Meanwhile, sales of the 777 had continued at a steady rate despite an economic slow-down which had the usual effect of reducing orders for other airliners. United deferred 122 Boeing deliveries in February 1992 with some delays in the delivery rate of the 777s. On the more positive side, Cathay Pacific placed orders for 11 777s, with options on a further 11 to be powered by the Rolls-Royce Trent engines. As already mentioned, Cathay was interested more in the longer range, high-capacity version, and retained the flexibility to add this later. At the end of 1992, China Southern placed an order for six 380-seat two-class 777s, taking the total order book to almost 120 aircraft with nearly 100 options.

In June 1993 Japan Air System (JAS) exchanged six of its previously ordered 747-

400s for seven 777s as part of a cost-cutting exercise, the first aircraft being delivered on 4 December 1996 and powered by PW4084 engines for operation on the domestic network. In May 1993 Continental Airlines ordered 92 Boeing airliners, with options on 98 more aircraft. This order included 10 GE-powered 777IGWs, plus 50 RB211-powered 757s and 30 767s. In November 1993 Gulf Air signed a letter of intent to buy up to 12 777s powered by the GE90 engines, but due to economic difficulties this order was not confirmed. Following a major fleet evaluation, Saudia selected Boeing as the major supplier in May 1994, with 12 Trent-powered 777-200s as part of the requirement, but government approval was required as well as the raising of the finance. By mid-1995 the 777 requirement had increased to 23 aircraft, the contract being signed with the selection of the GE90 engines in October 1995. Following some delays with confirming the financial details, the first 777-200 was handed over at Seattle on 22 December 1997, together with a 747-400, MD-11F and MD-90. On 14 December 1993 Korean Air confirmed an order for eight 777IGWs for services to Chicago and New York, later selecting the PW4090 engines, and options on a further eight which could include the stretched version. After placing an order for up to 20 777s in October 1991, Japan Airlines finally selected the P&W engine in January 1994, making Pratt & Whitney successful in selling its engines to all three Japanese airlines, making joint maintenance more practical. In November 1995 JAL added five 777-300s for domestic trunk routes, and the first -200 was handed over at Seattle on 16 February 1996.

In December 1993 Transbrasil ordered three 777s and confirmed the Trent engine the following February, but the order was cancelled in mid-1995 due to over-capacity. However, the airline signed a letter of intent for four 777-200IGWs in February 1998. In mid-1994 Singapore Airlines (SIA) confirmed its interest in the 777 amongst other aircraft, requiring up to eight Trent-powered aircraft to replace the earlier Airbus A310s starting in 1996, and in September 1995 was looking at a fleet mix of the 777-200IGW and -300. By August 1995 total firm orders had reached 164 777s, and soon after Egyptair ordered three PW4000-powered 777-200IGWs, the first being delivered in May 1997. In September 1995 ANA signed the contract for 10 777-300s to carry up to 480 passengers in a two-class layout, replacing the carrier's 747SRs on the high-density domestic routes. By this time ANA had confirmed orders for 18 777-200s, the first of which was delivered in October 1995. In November 1995 South

African Airways confirmed its interest in seven 777s, but continuing delays over the engine selection and offset agreements caused the contract to lapse, and it still had not materialised by mid-1998. SIA also confirmed its order for 34 777s, with options on a further 43 aircraft in November 1995, powered by the Rolls-Royce Trent engine, for deliveries between 1997 and 2004. This order included six aircraft with 10 options for Singapore Aircraft Leasing, and the first 777-200 for SIA was delivered on 6 May 1997 with service entry on 15 May.

1996 started well with an order from Malaysia Airlines (MAS) in January for 15 Trent-powered 777s, including five of the stretched -300s and options on another two 777s. This order included some 747-400s, and the new fleet was planned to increase frequencies and start new thinner routes to the Middle East, South Africa and South America. In March ILFC announced orders for 18 777-200/300s with options on two, all three of the engine manufacturers sharing in the order. The first Rolls-Royce Trent-engined 777-200 was handed over to Thai International Airways at the end of March, ready for service entry in June. Having overcome the earlier economic problems, United continued its support for Boeing by placing further orders in May 1996, the bulk of the order being for 15 777s with the possibility of increasing to 17, taking total commitment to 85 of the type by the airline, and including a majority of the stretched -300. The following month BA was considering adding further 757s and 777s, its backlog including 12 777-200s with 15 options with 44 757s in operation. Also in June China Southern was reported to be negotiating a lease for three more 777-200IGWs to add to the six GE-powered 777s already ordered and entering service. In November 1996 American placed an exclusive order with Boeing for up to 630 aircraft over a period of 20 years. This order included 12 firm 777-200IGWs with purchase rights on 38, firm orders for four CF6-powered 767-300ERs with purchase rights on 26, and firm orders for 12

RB211-powered 757-200s with purchase rights on 38. At this same time Air France received government approval to purchase 10 288-seat three-class 777-200IGWs powered by GE90s, with options on 10 more. This order replaced the earlier cancelled order for 767s and 737s, and the first aircraft was delivered in April 1998. Asiana confirmed its selection of the PW4000 series engines for the 10 777-200IGWs and 10 777-300s on order or option in November.

On 16 October 1997 the first 777-300 made its maiden flight from Everett powered by Rolls-Royce Trent 892 turbofans landing after a flawless 4hr 6min at Boeing Field flight test centre. The 777-300 is the largest twin-engined airliner, and the longest airliner in the world, one of the features being ground manoeuvring cameras mounted in the tail and under the fuselage. The launch customer for this version was Cathay Pacific. The major change of the -300 over the earlier version was a forward fuselage stretch of 5.3m and a rear cabin stretch of 4.8m giving 20% more passenger capacity. Every effort was made for this to be a minimum-change aircraft in order to keep costs down, except where changes had to be made because of the increased size. Type certification from both the FAA and JAA was achieved on 4 May 1998, with

the FAA also approving 180min EROPS. Cathay Pacific received its first 777-300 on 21 May. Unfortunately the PW4098-powered 777-300 was delayed due to problems with the engine during testbed runs, the first customer being Korean Air Lines which expected the first delivery in September 1998, but faced delays of over three months. Certification of the 436kN (98,000lb)-thrust PW4098 was finally achieved at the end of July 1998 with deliveries to KAL expected in time for services to commence in December. The deliveries of the PW4090-powered 777-300s to ANA were unaffected and started in July, with JAL taking delivery of the first of five PW4090-powered 777-300s on 28 July.

In November 1997, Delta confirmed its 10 options for 777-200s, adding a further 20 options along with rolling options for another 30 aircraft. Meanwhile, due to the worsening Asian economic crisis Asiana deferred deliveries of the 777s for about two years, Malaysia Airlines offered five Trent-powered 777 delivery positions to VASP and Thai Airways was hoping to defer some of the later deliveries. Even the financially strong SIA postponed delivery of three 777s due for delivery in late 1999. Also in November 1997, China Aviation Supplies

(CASC) ordered a number of 777s, 757s and 737s, with flag carrier Air China being allocated five of the eight 777-200IGWs. The remaining three 777s were allocated to China Southern to add to its fleet of six 777s. All five 757s were allocated to China Xinjiang Airlines.

In March 1998 Boeing was still promoting the 777X launch with a requirement for around 30 777-200Xs before go-ahead of the ultra-long-range derivative. Some 70% of the development work had been completed with assembly of the first -200X proposed to begin in August, followed by the longer -300X in December. The major requirement was from the now depressed Asian market for flights across the Pacific. Also, the longer the launch delay, the greater the loss of advantage over improved Airbus A340 developments, the A340-500 being ordered by SIA in May 1998, forcing Boeing to review the 777X programme. Work continued to refine the design and Rolls-Royce continued to develop the Trent 8104 which was expected to develop 454kN (102,000lb) of thrust with the first engine

running in December 1998. To provide additional thrust, Boeing was considering the use of a third tail-mounted engine in the 31 to 66.7kN (7,000 to 15,000lb) class to be used for additional take-off thrust as well as an APU.

Air Europe (Italy) signed a lease deal with ILFC in May 1998 for two 777-200ERs, as the 777-200IGW was now known, powered by PW4090 engines, for delivery in July and October 1999. Also in May, Continental changed four of its orders for 767-400ERs to 777-200ERs. In June 1998 Aeroflot Russian Airlines (ARIA) took delivery of the first of two 777-200ERs under a seven-year lease from ILFC.

In mid-1998 BA was considering buying a further 20 777s to add to the current fleet of 18 aircraft with 11 more on order and option. Having originally selected the GE90 engine, with the lack of further development investment in the engine BA was having to consider alternative engines, Rolls-Royce being its traditional supplier.

Above:
The first Boeing 777-300 N5014W powered by Rolls-Royce Trent engines, destined for delivery to Cathay Pacific after completion of the development flying, is seen taking-off from Boeing Field at Seattle in May 1998 on a further test flight. *Author*

Right:
The first of 10 PW4000-powered Boeing 777-381s, JA751A for ANA, is seen on the flight line at Everett in May 1998 being prepared for flight, and painted in a special commemorative colour scheme. *Author*

Appendicies

Specifications

	Boeing 757-300	Boeing 767-400ER	Boeing 777-300
Wing span (ft/m)	124.64/38.0	170.23/51.9	199.75/60.9
Wing area (sq ft/sq m)	1,951.5/181.3	3,129/290.7	4,607/428
Wing sweep (°)	25	31.5	31.6
Length (ft/m)	178.43/54.4	201.39/61.4	242/73.8
Height (ft/m)	44.61/13.6	55.43/16.9	60.35/18.4
Cabin length (ft/m)	141.60/43.17	153.57/46.82	193.68/59.05
Cabin width (ft/m)	11.07/3.53	15.06/4.72	19.3/5.87
Max seating	279	245	550
Cargo vol (cu ft/cu m)	2,387/67.6	-	-
Fuel capacity (US gal/ltr)	11,490/43,493	24,140/91,370	45,219/171,155
Max t/o weight (lb/kg)	270,000/122,470	449,064/204,120	658,625/299,375
Landing weight (lb/kg)	223,531/101,605	-	522,896/237,680
Zero fuel weight (lb/kg)	209,561/95,255	226,820/103,100	493,996/224,530
Max range (nm/km)	4,010/6,455	5,600/10,360	6,334/11,718
Cruise speed (kt)	505	-	499
Ceiling (ft)	42,000	-	43,100
Engines	R-R RB211-535E4B, P&W PW2043	P&W PW4062, GE CF6-80C2	R-R Trent 875, P&W PW4098, GE GE90-95B

United Airlines has always been a major operator of Boeing airliners, placing the launch order for the 767. In addition to the initial fleet of 18 767-200s, United also has in service or on order 27 767-300ERs. In recent years United has been changing its colour scheme, and 767-322ER N644UA is seen on finals at Hong Kong Kai Tak in April 1998. *Author*

123

Orders

Boeing 757 Programme Announced Orders
(31 March 1992)

Customer	Series	First Order	No	First Delivery	No	Engine	Remarks
Air 2000	757	12/12/86	1	27/4/87	1	R-R RB211-535E4	Remainder of fleet leased
Air Europa	757	25/4/88	2			R-R RB211-535E4	
Air Europe (UK)	757	2/7/82	14	30/3/83	14	R-R RB211-535E4	Ceased Operations
Air Holland	757	25/5/87	3	9/3/88	3	R-R RB211-535E4	Ceased Operations
America West	757	6/2/87	14	10/12/87	4	R-R RB211-535E4/B	
*American	757	25/5/88	91	17/7/89	56	R-R RB211-535E4B	535E4B Launch Customer
*Ansett Worldwide	757	7/10/87	19	15/2/89	13	R-R RB211-535E4	Not an operator
	757-200PF		3	26/7/89	3	R-R RB211-535E4	Package Freighter
Aries Leasing (Amex)	757	25/4/88	2	11/4/91	1	R-R RB211-535E4	
*Britannia	757-200	1991	6	11/4/92	1	R-R RB211-535E4	
*British Airways	757	31/8/78	42	25/1/83	39	R-R RB211-535C/E4	
*CAAC	757	20/1/87	33	22/9/87	13	R-R RB211-535E4	
*Condor	757	29/9/88	16	19/3/90	10	PW2040	
Continental	757	8/10/90	25				
*Delta	757	12/11/80	88	5/11/84	74	PW2037	
Eastern	757	31/8/78	25	22/12/82	25	R-R RB211-535C/E4	Ceased Operations
*El Al Israel	757	1/10/86	5	25/11/87	5	R-R RB211-535E4	
Electra Aviation	757	25/4/88	1			R-R RB211-535E4	Ex-Air Europe 1991
*Ethiopian	757-200	9/6/89	4	25/2/91	2	PW2040	
	757-200PF		1	24/8/90	1	PW2040	Package Freighter
*GPA Ltd	757-200	18/4/89	51	30/8/91	3	R-R RB211-535E4	
Icelandair	757	19/10/88	3	4/4/90	3	R-R RB211-535E4	
*Int'l Lease	757	18/6/86	35	1/4/87	14	PW2037/ R-R RB211-535E4	Not an operator
*LTU	757	25/8/83	9	25/5/84	9	R-R RB211-535C/E4	
Mexico-Govt	757	16/11/87	1	16/11/87	1	R-R RB211-535E4	
Monarch (UK)	757	19/2/81	7	21/3/83	7	R-R RB211-535E4/C-37	
Northwest	757	29/11/83	73	28/2/85	33	PW2037	
Republic	757	1/10/85	6	6/12/85	6	R-R RB211-535E4	Merged
Royal Air Maroc	757	5/2/86	2	15/7/86	2	PW2037	
Royal Brunei	757	30/5/85	3	6/5/86	3	R-R RB211-535E4	
Royal Nepal	757	17/2/86	1	9/9/87	1	R-R RB211-535E4	
	757-200M		1	15/9/88	1	R-R RB211-535E4	Combi
Shanghai Airlines	757	14/12/88	8	4/8/89	3	PW2037	
Singapore	757	31/5/83	4	12/11/84	4	PW2037	Disposed of
Sterling	757	13/1/89	3	2/8/90	3	R-R RB211-535E4	
Sunrock A/C Corp	757	25/4/88	2	19/6/91	1	R-R RB211-535E4	
Transavia	757-200	23/5/89	2	1993			
*United	757	26/5/88	90	24/8/89	54	PW2037	
United Parcel	757-200PF	21/12/85	55	17/9/87	25	PW2040/ R-R RB211-535 (20)	Package Freighter
US Air	757-200	30/3/92	15			R-R RB211	
Xiaman	757-200	27/10/89	3			R-R RB211-535E4	
TOTALS			**785**		**437**		

* Also has 767s either ordered or delivered.

Boeing 767 Programme announced orders
(31 March 1992)

Customer	Series	First Order	No	First Delivery	No	Engine	Remarks
Aeromaritime	767-200ER	17/1/89	2	26/7/90	2	PW4060	
	767-300ER	17/1/89	1	22/8/91	1	PW4060	
Air Algerie	767-300	1/5/89	3	28/6/90	3	CF6-80C2-B2	
Air Canada	767-200	11/7/79	10	30/10/82	10	PWJT9D-7R4D	
	767-200ER		9	18/10/84	9	PWJT9D-7R4D	
	767-300ER	31/8/89	9	1993		PW4060	
Air France	767-300ER	7/2/92	3				
Air Mauritius	767-200ER	19/1/87	2	5/4/88	2	CF6-80C2-B4	
Air New Zealand	767-200ER	3/7/84	3	3/9/85	3	CF6-80A2	
	767-300ER		4				
Air Pacific	767-300ER	9/10/90	1				
Air Zimbabwe	767-200ER	20/7/88	2	28/11/89	2	PW4056	
All Nippon Airways	767-200	1/10/79	25	25/4/83	25	CF6-80A	
	767-300		31	30/6/87	19	CF6-80C2-B2/B2F	
	767-300ER		5	36/6/90	3	CF6-80C2-B2F/B6	
American	767-200	15/11/78	13	4/11/82	13	CF6-80A	
	767-200ER		17	18/11/85	17	CF6-80A	
	767-300ER		40	19/2/88	19	CF6-80C2-B6	
Ansett Worldwide	767-200ER		3	1/5/90	3		
Leasing	767-300ER	16/11/88	4	13/12/91	4	PW4056	
Ansett (Australia)	767-200	17/3/80	5	7/6/83	5	CF6-80A	
Asiana	767-300	23/12/88	10	27/9/90	2	CF6-80C2-B2F	
	767-300ER		2		2		
Avianca (Colombia)	767-200ER	24/12/88	2	26/2/90	2	PW4056	
Braathens (Norway)	767-200	28/4/80	2	23/2/84	2	PWJT9D-7R4D	Not operating this type
Britannia	767-200	31/3/80	11	6/2/84	11	CF6-80A	
British Airways	767-300ER	14/8/87	25	8/2/90	17	R-R RB211-524H	
CAAC	767-200ER	23/5/85	10	8/10/85	6	PW4052/PWJT9D-7R4E	
Canadian	767-200	21/12/78	2	4/3/83	2	PWJT9D-7R4D	Not operating this type
	767-300ER		14	15/4/88	12	CF6-80C2-B6	
China Airlines	767-200	20/3/80	2	20/12/82	2	PWJT9D-7R4D	
CIAF-ONE	767-300ER	31/7/91	3				
Condor	767-300ER	27/6/91	13		3		
Delta	767-200	15/11/78	15	25/10/82	15	CF6-80A	
	767-300		30	7/11/86	23	CF6-80A/A2	
	767-300ER		14	9/6/90	9	PW4060	
Egyptair	767-200ER	12/1/84	3	20/7/84	3	PWJT9D-7R4E	
	767-300ER		2	15/8/89	2	PW4060	
El Al Israel	767-200	18/3/81	2	12/7/83	2	PWJT9D-7R4D	
	767-200ER		2	26/3/84	2	PWJT9D-7R4D	
Ethiopian	767-200ER	16/12/82	3	18/5/84	3	PWJT9D-7R4E	
EVA Air	767-300ER	6/10/89	6	30/5/91	2	CF6-80C2-B6F	
GATX/CL Air	767-200ER	24/5/89	1	25/1/91	1	CF6-80A2	
GPA Ltd Leasing	767-200ER	18/4/89	1		1	PW4000	
	767-300ER		7	28/2/91	7	PW4000	
	767-TBD		32				
Gulf Air	767-300ER	8/9/88	16	13/4/89	10	CF6-80C2	Began service with leased aircraft
Int'l Lease	767-200	19/2/86	1	25/8/87	1	CF6-80A/A2	
	767-200ER		4	29/5/86	4	CF6-80A/C2-B4	
	767-300ER		19	12/3/91	5	CF6-80C2-B4	
Japan Airlines	767-200	29/9/83	3	22/7/85	3	PWJT9D-7R4D	
	767-300		13	9/9/86	13	PWJT9D-7R4D	
Kuwait	767-200ER	18/9/84	3	20/3/86	3	PWJT9D-7R4E	

LAM	767-200ER	1/8/90	1			PW4000		
Lauda Air	767-300ER	21/4/87	4	29/4/88	2	PW4060		
LOT	767-200ER	4/11/88	2	21/4/89	2	CF6-80C2-B4		
	767-300ER		1	21/8/90	1	CF6-80C2-B6		
LTU	767-300ER	21/1/88	3	2/2/89	3	PW4060		
Malev	767-200ER	21/2/91	2					
Martinair	767-300ER	11/3/88	6	21/9/89	6	PW4060		
Piedmont	767-200ER	25/7/86	9	21/5/87	9	CF6-80C2-B2	Now USAir	
Polaris/Gulf Air	767-300ER	27/4/88	2	13/6/88	2	CF6-80C2-B4	Polaris — not an operator	
Qantas	767-200ER	7/9/83	7	3/7/85	7	PWJT9D-7R4B		
	767-300ER		13	30/8/88	12	CF6-80C2-B6		
SAS	767-200ER	18/1/88	2	11/5/90	2	PW4056		
	767-300ER		14	29/3/89	14	PW4060		
TACA (El Salvador)	767-200	22/5/86	1	22/5/86	1	CF6-80A		
	767-300ER		1		1			
Trans World Airlines	767-200	5/12/79	10	22/11/82	10	PWJT9D-7R4D		
Transbrasil	767-200	30/7/81	3	23/6/83	3	CF6-80A		
United	767-200	14/7/78	19	19/8/82	19	PWJT9D-7R4D		
	767-300ER	19/5/89	26	18/4/91	6	PW4060		
USAir	767-200ER	20/6/91	2	20/6/91	2	CF6-80C2		
Varig	767-200ER	18/3/86	6	2/7/87	6	CF6-80C2-B2		
	767-300ER	20/3/89	4	22/12/89	4	CF6-80C2-B2		
Totals			**603**		**422**			

Sales Update

Boeing has ceased to supply regular published figures of sales and deliveries. The data below is taken from published sources and therefore is not as complete as would be hoped. Efforts have been made to avoid counting sales of second-hand aircraft, or leases, and there will almost certainly be some duplication of the new orders by the lease companies, as it is not always clear where those aircraft are to be allocated.

Boeing 757 announced orders
from 1992 up to 7 September 1998

Sales and delivery totals up to 31 July 1998

Airline	Model	Order date	No	First delivery	Engines	Options/Leased
ILFC	-200	12.92	19	-		5 options
Britannia	-200ER	1.93	7	-	RB211-535E4	-
Air Seychelles	-200ER	-	1	3.93	RB211-535E4	-
Continental	-200	5.93	50	-	RB211-535E4	-
Ambassador	-	-	2	5.93	-	leased
China Southern	-200	7.93	4	-	-	leased
UPS	-200PF	11.93	10	-	RB211-535E4	-
ILFC	-200	12.93	5	-	-	-
Transaero	-200	-	2	4.94	-	leased + 2 in 1995
Baikal	-200	-	1	6.94	RB211-535E4	ILFC lease
China SW	-200	.94	12	.94	-	-
ATA	-200	9.94	2	-	PW2037	ILFC lease
ATA	-200	9.94	6	-	PW2037	-
United	-200	4.95	5	-	PW2037	-
LAPA	-200	-	1	28.9.95	-	leased
Uzbekistan	-200	10.95	1	-	-	-
CAA Turkmenistan	-200	10.95	2	-	-	-
TWA	-200	2.96	20	1.8.96	PW2037	10 ILFC leased
Finnair	-200ER	4.96	4	9.97	-	ILFC lease
Flying Colours	-200ER	4.96	4	26.2.97	RB211-535E4	leased

Airline	Model	Order date	No	First delivery	Engines	Options/Leased
United	-200	5.96	5	-	PW2037	-
Condor	-300ER	9.96	12	-	PW.2043	12 options
ILFC	-200ER	9.96	5	-	-	-
BA	-200ER	9.96	3	-	RB211-535E4	-
Delta	-200	9.96	4	-	PW2037	ILFC lease
American	-200	11.96	12	-	RB211-535E4	ILFC lease + 38 options
Mexicana	-200ER	-	2	1.97	PW2037	ILFC lease
Continental	-200	3.97	16	-	RB211-535E4	-
Icelandair	-200	6.97	2	1.98	RB211-535E4	-
Icelandair	-300ER	6.97	2	-	RB211-535E4	8 options
Delta	-200	3.97	5	-	PW2037	20 options
USAF	C-23A	-	4	4.98	-	-
FEAT	-200	11.97	5	.99	-	5 options
ILFC	-200ER	9.97	6	-	-	-
Xianjiang	-200	11.97	5	-	-	-
Arkia	-300ER	7.98	2	-	-	-

Total orders 922, total deliveries 810

Boeing 767 Announced Orders
from 1992 up to 31 August 1998

Airline	Model	Order date	No	First delivery	Engines	Options/Leased
Mozambique	-200ER	1992	2	-	-	-
Eva Air	-300ER	1992	2	-	CF6-80C2	-
Malev	-300ER	1992	1	5.92	-	-
ILFC	-	12.92	10	-	-	5 options
Malev	-200ER	1993	2	-	-	-
UPS	-300F	1.93	30	12.10.95	CF6-80C2	-
Leisure	-300ER	1993	2	-	CF6-80C2	ILFC lease
Air Pacific	-300ER	1993	1	-	-	-
Continental	-300ER	5.93	30	-	-	-
ANA	-300	10.93	2	-	-	-
Japan	E-767	11.93	2	11.3.98	CF6-80C2	+ 2 more leased
Aeroflot	-300ER	1.94	4	-	-	leased
Kazakhstan	-300ER	1.94	4	-	PW4056	+ 3 more in 1995
Britannia	-300ER	12.94	4	-	-	4 options
Asiana	-300F	1995	2	8.96	-	-
China Yunnan	-300ER	1.95	3	-	RB211-524G/H	-
Alitalia	-300ER	8.95	3	-	-	leased
KLM	-300ER	6.95	7	-	-	leased
Lauda Air	-300ER	8.95	1	-	PW4060	4 in service
Uzbekistan	-300ER	10.95	2	-	-	-
American	-300ER	11.96	4	-	CF6-80C2	26 options
Air Seychelles	-300ER	12.96	1	-	-	-
Sobelair	-300ER	1.97	2	1.98	-	-
Delta	-400ER	3.97	21	2000	-	24 options
Delta	-300ER	3.97	10	-	-	10 options
Continental	-400ER	6.97	30	2000	-	4 in 5.98
ILFC	-400ER	9.97	5	-	-	-
BA	-300ER	6.97	3	4.98	RB211-525G/H	-
United	-300ER	6.97	8	-	PW400	-
LanChile	-300ER	6.97	3	-	-	-
Asiana	-300ER	8.97	2	-	-	+ 2 more 1.98
ILFC	-300ER	9.97	7	-	-	-
Varig	-300ER	9.98	6	1999	CF6-80C2	-

Total orders 828, total deliveries 709

Boeing 777 Announced Orders
from 1990 up to 31 August 1998

Airline	Model	Order date	No	First delivery	Engines	Options/Leased
United Airlines	-200	10.90	34	5/95	PW4000	-
All Nippon Airways	-200	12.90	15	1996	PW4073A	-
Eural Air	-200	6.91	2	-	-	
Thai International	-200	6.91	8	-	R-R Trent	6
British Airways	-200	8.91	15	-	GE90	15
Lauda Air	-200	12.91	4	-	GE90	-
Japan Airlines	-200	1.91	10	-	-	10
Cathay	-200	3.92	11	9.5.96	Trent	-
ILFC	-200	12.92	6	-	-	2 options
China Southern	-200	12.92	6	28.12.95	GE90	-
Continental	-200ER	5.93	10	-	GE90	+ 4 more 5.98
JAS	-200	6.93	7	4.12.96	PW4084	-
Korean	-200ER	12.93	8	-	PW4090	8 options
Saudia	-200ER	5.94	23	22.12.97	GE90	-
Cathay	-300ER	6.95	7	21.5.98	Trent	11 options
Korean	-300ER	6.95	4	12.98	PW4098	-
Thai	-300ER	6.95	6	31.3.96	Trent	-
Egyptair	-200ER	9.95	3	2.97	PW4000	-
ANA	-200ER	9.95	3	31.10.95	PW4084	-
ANA	-300ER	10.95	10	28.7.98	PW4090	5 options
JAL	-200	11.95	5	-	PW4000	-
SIA	-200ER	11.95	28	6.5.97	Trent	33 options
Singapore A/c Leasing	-200ER	11.95	6	-	-	10 options
Malaysia	-200ER	1.96	10	23.4.97	Trent	-
Malaysia	-300ER	1.96	5	-	Trent	2 options
ILFC	-200/-300	3.96	18	-	-	2 options
United	-200/-300ER	5.96	15	-	PW4000	-
American	-200ER	11.96	12	-	-	38 options
Air France	-200ER	11.96	10	4.98	GE90	10 options
Asiana	-200ER	11.96	10	-	PW4000	orders and options
Asiana	-300ER	11.96	10	-	PW4000	orders and options
Delta	-200	11.97	10	-	Trent	20 options
Air China	-200ER	11.97	5	-	PW4077	-
China South	-200ER	11.97	3	-	GE90	-
Transbrasil	-200ER	2.98	4	-	Trent	-
Air Europe	-200ER	5.98	2	7.99	PW4090	ILFC lease
Aeroflot	-200ER	-	2	6.98	-	ILFC lease
BA	-200ER	8.98	16	-	-	16 options
Varig	-200ER	9.98	4	-	GE90	4 options

Total orders 392, total deliveries 146